Stop the Children from Crying

a river of tears.

by Kathy Garbe

Stop the Children from Crying a River of Tears

Copyright © 2011 by Kathy Garbe

Library of Congress Control Number: 2011942389
ISBN: 978-1466494237

Websites: http://KathyGarbe.com
http://Facebook.com/StopTheChildrenFromCryin
g

Front Cover artwork by
Judy Smith/JAGS

Endorsement

While walking the Red Road and performing our Native sacred healing ceremonies I often encounter souls seeking their spiritual path. We are taught that there are many paths to the Creator, and you must choose with your heart. All loving paths led to the same mountain top. In her writings, Kathy, embodies this with her beautiful words and stories. She teaches that loving and respecting one another despite our differences is the first step on life's sacred journey.

Rev. Barry White Crow /Spiritual Advisor for Sacred Grounds

Dedication

I would like to dedicate this book to the two men in my life.

My wonderful husband and partner in life Michael, he is like my breath when I forget to breath. He gives me the inspiration I need when I throw up my hands and say I'm done no more. He listens as I read out loud and then say WELL? Unsure if he should answer or not.

He has learned to turn his hearing on and off at the drop of a hat...but all things said and done my heart and soul are his. He has been a trooper through this whole ordeal, and I give him my thanks and love for understanding me and always being there at my time of need. Honey I love you.

To Richard, my son whom has always been called Andy after his grandfather. A beautiful name you carry for both your father and grandfather. How proud I was the day you were born, all twelve pounds of you. You came into this world with a big bang, and you have given our world a master piece with the gentleness and love you share for all beings and animals alike. In case I have not told you enough I love you, and I am so very proud of you.

Blessings,

Kathy Garbe

Chapters

Acknowledgments --- vii

Introduction --- 1

1 - Who is the Light? -- 5

2 - Consequences -- 10

3 - Changes -- 15

4 - Fear The Downfall of Mankind ------------------------ 18

5 - My Awakening --- 23

6 - Respecting Self --- 29

7 - Let The Light Shine ------------------------------------- 33

8 - The Store/Complaint Department ------------------- 40

9 - Tired of Trying, Tired of Being, Tired of Life -- 46

10 - Where Does a Person Go From There ------------- 51

11 - How Much Can One Person Take -------------------- 53

12 - Confused --- 61

13 The Time Has Come --------------------------------------- 65

14 - Kids There is Something to be Said About Them
--- 71

15 - At Any Given Time -------------------------------------- 75

16 - You Know... You Just Know ---------------------------- 79

17 - What Am I Going To Be When I Grow Up ------ 83

18 -Can It Change? How and When Will it Change 90

19 -Spirit --95

20 -I Am Scared ---103

21 -Children and Prayer -----------------------------------105

22 -Trying Times --109

23 -There is a Story to be Told----------------------------- 114

24 -Nightmares / Night Terrors---------------------------119

25 -Prayer of Grace -- 128

26 -Spirit Steps In-- 133

27 -Growth --- 137

28 -Suicide --- 141

29 -Today is the day... ------------------------------------147

30 -The End Or Is It Just The Beginning ------------ 153

Acknowledgments

First, my thanks to everyone who has helped me along the way with a special thank you to all my students who have given me the courage to proceed forward on my Spiritual path.

To Barbara Hicks for reading and helping to see parts that I needed to expand on and for being a friend in times of need.

A big thank you to my good friend and artist Judy Smith/JAGS for drawing the most inspirational book cover I have ever seen. It makes me melt inside every time I look at it and feel what it represents in our world today. Thank you for the insight with your beautiful drawing.

To Barb Anderson, all her help and patience with the computer, as I struggled, and helping to put my book together as it was meant to be.

To Michael, my husband for seeing me through the years it took me to write this book and to my children, Lucinda, Tina, Christy and Andy for their love and support.

I especially would like to thank all those who have read my first book, Butterfly Within, and expressed enjoyment of my work and how they found themselves inside my book.

Last but not least my thanks to God our Father for being in my life and instilling in me the beauty of faith.

Introduction

As I tell this story I am pledged by many thoughts of my own, plus Spirit. The good and the bad, knowing its neither all good nor bad. It is left up to us to make the decisions in our own lives of how we want to live it. I know how many times in my own life I have changed, I have grown, I have seen the difference between the light and dark and I know without a shadow of a doubt that Spirit has led me, guided me with the grace of my intuition into a much better needed space then I was in before. Without Spirit and God I would have been lost. God plays the most important role in my life as in this book. We need to send a message to all our children near and far that God is standing by our side. It is time to make contact with him as our provider, not only for our sake but for the sake of all children. We must reconnect with him to allow the light to shine brighter in each and every one of us.

As I have said many times over the energy in our world is trembling and moving way too fast for us to keep up with it. If we cannot keep up with it how can we expect our children to keep up? It is them that I fear for. It is your child and my child that I worry so about. They have been moving so fast through this world of ours that they have forgotten how to pray. Even worse they were never taught to pray, to make that connection with God. How can they go through this world not armed in LOVE? How will they survive in a world where they were not taught the basics, never given the foundation on how to reach our Heavenly Father?

We have been selfish in our cross roads and in to much of a hurry to grab and reach all new heights, in getting what it is we want in our lives, instead of seeking out the goodness and loving part and watching it nurture into being. We have been what everyone expected us to be, running, never stopping to look around. Time is always of the essence and never enough of it. We have heard all the excuses, we know them all by heart, we have used them to make ourselves feel better about what it is we do. We have come to the part in our lives where we are tired... We want more of the good loving energy that we have misplaced. It is time to take a good hard look at what we are doing in our own lives and how we affect other lives. How we can once again connect to the inner light that lies within each and every one of us waiting patiently for us to seek it out. To connect not only with our light but with God our Father that so graciously gives of us the light we seek.

As you read the words in this book you will feel the wisdom and strength that spirit has graciously given to us. It will awaken the knowledge that lies within you. It will help you to achieve where it is you wish to be and where it is you know you want to be in this life, your life. So my friends enjoy what you read, seek the wisdom; acknowledge what you seek, and most of all find the love that you so rightly deserve.

Blessings to all,

Kathy Garbe

*The future depends on what
We do in the present.*

By Unknown

Chapter 1

Who is the Light?
Where can we find it?
How do we get some?

As I am getting ready to sit and write I see it coming to me or am I going to it. A desk waits, a beautiful antique quaint old desk with the chair pulled out waiting. The only thing on the desk is paper and a quill and one lone beautiful red rose in a crystal vase. As I walk closer I feel the urge, the same urge that has been calling me since I wrote my last book. Yet this urge is necessary for my very existence on this plane. It's as if the words are coming at such a fast and powerful rate and yet so confusing because of the insistence, the push, that I sit and that I write. I see myself sit nervously, for faith in myself has never been one of my strongest points in life.

I grew up not remembering a lot of my childhood and I often wonder why. I always feel so alone and different. I never seemed to fit in. Was it any one's fault? No! I'm not going there, putting the blame on others, for what good does that do? Why do I have flash backs? Why can't I remember grade school? Why do I see the bad the hurt? Not only see but still remember, still feel the pain. It's so real, why doesn't it go away so I can be happy? Why am I so sad? Why do I cling to the love of the light? So many questions fill my head as I feel the light and know the safety it has brought to me and my children.

I look back like a slow old fashion movie playing in my head as I remember making my first holy communion. All dressed up in white. My beautiful white dress, white patent leather shoes, and ruffled socks, I remember my first little white purse, my first rosary and looking down at my little white bible, my veil covering my hair. I felt so special walking down the aisle, yet I found myself looking at my feet afraid to look up. I was afraid the priest would look at me and ask me a question. I wanted to be there, yet I wanted to be invisible. Somewhere inside of me was opening up for I knew without a shadow of a doubt I had been touched, not by the priest or the host we had to let melt in our mouth, but by something, someone, very special... the man who hung on the cross for us. I didn't like seeing him like that, and I asked him how many people have to suffer before they realize pain is not the answer. I felt, him smile at me, and I felt his touch. Love shot through me at that moment. I still feel those tears of joy, knowing what I saw and what I felt. I'm not saying I understood, yet at that time I thought I did. I was an innocent, young child, open to receive LOVE.

Did I like going to church (mass?) NO! It was too complicated. People were angry and very fearful. They dressed up in all their finest, the men in their suits and the women in their dresses and hats. The colognes and perfumes worn were too much for me to breathe in. I was forever holding my breath as my breathing was not always up to par, for you see I had asthma. The benches were too hard, the service too long, and we could not understand a word that was said, as they spoke in Latin. If we ever tried to leave early a priest would be waiting for us on the steps outside the church doors sending us right back inside with the fear of God in us.

As I recollect my brother, and I use to walk to church together, and he would go off and play hooky while I had to go to church. He would meet up with me on the walk home just in time to let our parents know we went to church just like we were told. Somehow, I always felt I got the short end of that deal.

I think back on those times and how I hated Sundays. I didn't like going too mass. I didn't like the feel of the people, so angry, gossipy, always checking everyone else out. I felt little in their eyes and very insecure and as much as I disliked Sundays, Saturday was my day of fear. Saturday was the day we went to confession and was the day panic sent in. You can't have communion and be saved unless you go to confession. Who made these rules up anyway? I must confess my sins. What sins did I have? I was but a child.... What was I to confess? I was just a little girl trying to be good. I wasn't trying to be bad. However, I had to confess something of my wrong doings, so I would make up a lie in order to confess. I didn't understand then nor now do I agree with such fear based religions. But I must confess some of my best times were sitting in the church when it was almost empty because then and only then could I communicate my love and my misery to the man on the cross. I knew he understood.

I had no one I could open up to in my family as I was the oldest girl of six children. My parents were busy taking care of all of us, and they were not church goers back then. However, they believed that we should be brought up with religion. I always wished we went to church as a family, a Childs dream to be like everyone else, one that I made come true when I had my own family. Did my children feel the same way as I did as a child? I don't know because I never asked them. I only knew that they had to know who God is and feel the light as I did, to know God personally, to give them the foundation my parents gave me. Today, I thank my parents for the wisdom of giving me my foundation.

Religion has its good points, its goodness it shows us how to pray, and who to pray to. Yet some go as far as to tell us what to wear, what to say, and who to speak to, and how to act. When we're in search of answers, it's a church we go to first, looking for our family unity. We open up our hearts and minds, and somehow we get so caught up that we forget who we are. We are God's child. We are made of his love. We shine with his light. He is forever watching over us and comes when we ask. It is so natural to go to a church searching. We want his love desperately. We are willing to do whatever it takes. Find the right place... Grow... yet do not get caught up in its fear or bitterness toward the next church for then you are not allowing the light of God to shine within you. If you have anger at other religions or churches or feel your God is better than theirs. How can he be better when there is only one? Years ago I was once told by someone we had different Gods, and I was going to burn in hell for laying on hands while doing healing work (Reiki) on someone who laid in the hospital in a coma. How could he attack me for calling on God for this healing, something that is used in many hospitals today? When I was confronted, I looked at him and said, "I am not going to fight about your God and my God, because I believe in an all loving God, yours and mine, which are one and the same." This is a God that hears and heals us when we ask. I do not have to know every quote in the bible to connect with God or Spirit as this man who is throwing quotes out at me. We are his children, and he is in every one of us. I believe if you have Love and Faith all things are possible and will be answered in his time and place. We must believe..., and we need to reach out of our comfort zone and know without a shadow of a doubt that God is with us at every turn of our lives. Sometimes the ones that yell the loudest do not always win.

There is no path to peace.

Peace is the path.

By Unknown

Chapter 2

Consequences

Families grow up differently in religion, ethics, rules, personality, fear, happiness. Some are quiet, the deep thinkers, or are they just afraid to stand up and speak their minds? Others are loud and scream and thump their fists in our faces because their truth is the only one, for they are right, and we are wrong. They are the know - it - all's, the ones we try to stay away from yet get caught up in because we can't run fast enough. They are all around us. You can feel the tragedy. You can feel the fear. You feel yourself cave in because it's just so much easier to go along than to fight. After awhile you start to believe, and you start to feel the power of hate, the unjust in the world. Words are only words but after words come pain. After pain comes closure for those you lash out at, and not the kind of closure that's good but the kind that shuts you down. You feel lost and believe you will never be saved and happy again. This comes from abuse, and abuse is all around us and still in many of our very lives this day. We abuse ourselves. Others abuse us, and we allow it. We do not reach out to help or be helped. We're too afraid. We must mind our own business. We feel we're not strong enough? Some of us find it is just easier to go along with it. However, at the same time we are filled with anger, hatred and a knowing truth that we are alone. We are tired and scared, weak and run into the ground. Where do we go? How do we walk away? How do we start over? No one wants me. No one loves me. I'm all alone. I'm afraid, like a wounded puppy. You can abuse a puppy, but they always come back for love.

We search love out anyway we can. We just want to be loved. It hurts to love, so let's turn it off. The feelings, the tenderness, let's beat ourselves up. Let's help whom ever, whatever but not ourselves. Let's build the wall and put the hurt behind it. You know who you are and how it's done. The stronger the walls the less you feel the pain. Don't let them down, don't let them slip because if you do you will feel the pain once again. You may even have to trust.

These words slide out of my hand, writing so quickly. It's hard to understand and feel, yet I feel the emptiness and the pain I went through when I finally learned how I must release the locks on my heart. I had been hurt badly not once, not twice but many times over, and each time I thought my world was coming to an end. The pain I felt, the mistrust, the hurt, can hurt and sadness kill a person? Only by ones own hand. Nevertheless the mind body and soul is tortured, as if there were real whips and chains. The scars are very real even if not on the outside they are there deeply hidden within for no one to see.

How can a body survive you ask? By believing in God and the light that saves and believing in you as being a vital part of God. As our father, he holds us closely watching over us as we walk the path of life. He does not choose you to go through this, yet he is so proud of the strength you have developed to continue to search to walk closer to him. He is your provider, our Father and your best friend. He comes when you call. He lays his hands upon you for healing and cleansing. He gives you that urge, that strength, if only you would turn to him and call out his name. Let him know he is wanted. He takes nothing from you, but gives of all his Love. His light surrounds you. He guides you with a tender hand. You are the one who strays. You are the one that shall suffer the consequences of your actions. There is a power within each, but you must find the true power, the power of good, the power of life, and the power of love.

When the words stopped tumbling out I was shaken. Wow... how can I put this in a book? What will people think?

If the truth be known people will listen. If they listen, they will hear, if they hear they will once again open their hearts and find their way back to me, to the light that saves.

Chapter 3

Changes

As I sit this day, my desk looks a little lonely as it has been waiting patiently for me to settle into its precious chair. I look at the quill (pen), and I think back over the last couple months. The urge to write was there yet the time seemed to have disappeared. That is one of our biggest complaints. No time, too busy, too much on my calendar, I'm tired, sleepy. Excuses, we all know what they are and how to use them. We surely do not benefit by them for they keep us behind schedule and make us feel guilty for what it is we are not doing or should have done. We spend more time trying to defend ourselves to ourselves and anyone else that will listen. We are the ones who administer the burdens and the hardships. We can put the blame else, where but when it comes right on back to us, we must accept our guilt and learn to move around it.

Change a big word, a hard word for no one likes change, especially our bodies and our minds. There is a control issue going on here, and it happens to be going on inside each of us whether you are aware of it or not. There is not one of us that likes change. Change takes us out of our comfort zone. It's not comfortable, and it's very scary. Did we say scary? Yes, we did because you thought you knew who you were, and now you're going to change what it took you so long to accomplish and accept. If the truth be known, we really do want change. We're tired of the old us and want more. Here lies the dilemma. If you want more and you want change, then you have to work at it. You must see it happening step by painful step. Painful you say! Now I have to think about it awhile. What are you thinking about? Wouldn't it be painful not to make some changes in your life? How boring and unhappy we would be if we did not allow new and exciting things to enter our lives. Let's go back to the work part. How much work did you say was involved? Are you backing out already? Do you see where this is taking you? To the original no time, too busy, right back to the start. So OK be miserable if that's what really makes you happy or let's get off our duffs and let's see what life has to offer us. One step at a time, that's all that's asked of you. Just one step at a time. We spend more time talking ourselves out of things. Why not take the step and see where the journey leads.

Now that's exciting! I feel like you're in my head, in my thoughts.

We are in all thoughts. We see them as the energy of time, of worry, of excuses, of fear, yet we see the thought patterns of knowledge, excitement, of newness, of want. It's all their mingled together. You need to separate your thought patterns and stop confusing yourself. See what it is you want. Know it by thought, see it as it is happening and then go forward and work it out one step at a time. Don't rush for we do not want you going backwards or quitting. Take your time, feel the energy of newness, of wholeness and bring it into your thought pattern, into your mind, your body and your spirit. Let yourself become awakened by the new energy and enjoy the wonderment of feeling as one. The pattern can be changed one by one to complete you as a whole.

You get to choose the time, the place and the commitment. The choice is yours and always has been. We are here to assist you now and always.

The words you have read above were written in 2005 and 2006 and throughout the book, you will find other parts of the story mixed in together as a whole. Spirit speaks to me in many different ways, and as I translate them, you will see the difference. You will find my words in normal writing, and Italic will be words of Spirit. Words below were written 2008-2009

If you judge people you have

no time to love them.

By Mother Theresa

Chapter 4

Fear The Downfall of Mankind

You have heard us when we call. We have tried to connect several times child and you sit like a log not letting us in. We know you have heard us and yet you did not come.

I wasn't ready. I didn't feel like I could connect correctly.

There is no correctly. There just is. Come to us with an

open mind and heart and we will do the rest.

But if I am not feeling up to par, I feel like I can't reach you.

This is nonsense, you are just afraid.

Afraid of what?

Your journey!

Am I ready to take this so called journey?

Your fear is speaking again. The reason you think you are not ready is because you are afraid.

Afraid of what I asked once again?

The outcome....

Even though I don't know what the outcome will be?

Exactly, our point! Fear has always been and will always be the downfall of mankind. It is our most disheartening difficult obstruction that we have to contend with. It just never goes away. People use it like a bandage. They hide under it and use it to cover up the mess of what it has done to their lives.

Fear F E A R it's just four little letters strung together. Take the F away and you have another word E.A.R. ear. Now that's an important word, a part of your body. Something that

God gave you to hear all the beauty in the world. Without your ears, you would miss out on some of God's most precious creations of the world. Now that's a mighty big gift for someone who is so fearful. We want you to think about that the next time FEAR seeps into your being.

My suggestion to you is to push fear aside and walk right on through it, pass it up and do not let it control you and your vessel.

Now there is another word for you, vessel. You notice we did not say the body. Too many of you dislike the body you look at every day. You condemn it, complain about it and abuse it. If you thought of yourself not as a body but as a vessel, would you not treat it better?

Your car is a vessel of sorts. Do you not treat it with kindness, oil changes, rotate tires, car wash and wax, inside and out, music to enjoy the ride, smells, so the interior feels like new? Does this not feel familiar to you? Do you not feed yourself, change your clothes, shower every day, and listen to music, smell of perfume or cologne so you appeal to others?

The difference is that you usually talk to your car nicely. Give it a pat or two. Feel proud of its purchase for it belongs to you. I can see your chest puff while talking about your baby while strutting like a peacock.

Now let's talk about you, your vessel. Wouldn't it feel wonderful to treat yourself the same way? Be proud of who you are. Talk nicely too and about yourself. See your body as your vehicle and praise yourself.

You are a good person, a beautiful person, God's child.

You know I have it from the greatest authority that God has never and will never produce a child who is ugly or unloved. All his children are beautiful. They come into this world with beauty and what happens to them afterward is not always there doing, or is it?

The culprit lies within the continuance of this world. To live too fast, to want too much, and to be selfish with giving of what matters to the vessel that God has given you.

Chapter 5

My Awakening

As I wake to write yet another chapter I look back at how all of this began.

My Spiritual teacher told me I would be writing a few books, Yes, I remember that, yet it was such a long time ago. Since then so much has happened. Am I the same person? Can I continue this journey, even though I have never had a writing lesson in my life? Can I tell the story the way it is supposed to be heard? I read other books, and I fall into them and wish I could tell this story like they have told theirs. Beauty in their words, the knowledge of writing and pulling their readers in to their world, these people know how to write. That's why they call them writers. The words flow with beauty, and they form the book so eloquently that you the reader becomes part of it. They know how it's done. So why do I sit here trying to write a book knowing that I am not a writer, and I do not know where to start or when to finish. When is a book finished anyway?

Here, I go again thinking too much. That has been my delay in the process of this book and in writing this book. This book is what I have been seeing and hearing in my head for so long, yet I have no knowledge of what words are going to be written for the entirety of it. Confusing, you bet it is, that is why I have waited seven long years of starting and stopping and starting and stopping again. Knowing that I must write and finish this book because I have been told to, not by my spiritual teacher yet very much by my teacher, the one I look to for answers to my problems, questions that need answers, the one that we all go to in times of healing and prayer. I have a connection with him that would seem unique, yet it is a very common connection that we all have but we all tend not to use it, unless we are in dire straits. Sound familiar? Yep, you all know who I'm talking about and yet too afraid to talk about it.

Now mind you, I am not a bible thumper, but I do take a peek into it every now and then looking for answers or comfort. I'm not a big church-goer yet I do find comfort going to church because that is supposedly where the big guy lives. Did I make mention that I teach meditation classes, not for the title of new age, you see there is nothing new about meditating, for they even meditate in the temples. What I do is pray, and prayer is older than all of us put together. Prayer is the connection to life. So who am I? I have no title. I like to think God connected to me because I am a common person. I have never ever given up on him and I have always searched him out for others that they too would learn to make that wonderful connection so they could go forth in life.

I have become more realistic with the unity of being, of who I am and what I can do to help others in the pursuit of happiness. Many times over it was and has been within my reach to help teach people how they can help themselves while helping others in return.

WOW a lot of words. What does all that mean? It simply means that we all have the ability within ourselves to help ourselves while always looking out for others. Do onto others as you yourself would want done unto you, not the perfect quote but close enough.

Again how did I get here and what did it take? It took a lot of heartache and tears, a divorce which led to a broken family, misery of misconception, trust and bafflement of life. We were all lost and confused. I knew I had to find happiness myself before I could help my children. We were all unhappy in the lives we led, and I took the only step, I knew that could help turn this around. I started to take steps to find that connection I so longed for, and my connection to God.

What a journey it has become. I have learned so much and yet have so much to learn. The learning never stops but what I have found out along the way is that the

25

fear can sometimes be the winner. What an ugly statement to make and yet the truth of it be told, every day it takes a lot of will power not to let the fear seep in and not to allow it to ruin or control our lives.

Fear grabs hold, and we have to wrestle with it to let us go. Like a hand that reaches out and grabs on to your throat, and you have to shake it off or it wraps around you and smothers you until you can't breathe and then the illness appears and shuts us down for repairs. Sounds like our vessels need some work. But as always, you need a good mechanic that knows how to gently put you back together again while learning the process of staying whole.

Like many people, I like to hide my feelings and tough it out. If someone hassles me, I let them push just so far before I take a stand. I am not a fighter and despise yelling, screaming and fighting. Even so, like the rest of us, it is something that people get used to right along with foul language. They spit those words out like there is no tomorrow. I wonder sometimes if they really know what those words mean and do they even care? Some may and others just don't care. It's about the power they feel when they use foul language and yell at the top of their lungs, the power it gives them to overpower someone else. You do know the one who yells the loudest is not always RIGHT. Let me tell you about fate and belief about knowing the difference between right and wrong. You have all been taught to give thanks and yet how soon you all forget. Grateful for the day and hurrying about for the outcome of reward stopping for no one and running over everyone to get to the finish line only to find out you are alone in the end. That is what happens to those that try to control others. Whether it is with words, force, fear or betrayal it does not matter for you will always stand alone in this cold cruel world that you have forced upon another. You may feel the benefit, but you will never be the one that people flock to, for you give of only mistrust and refuse to listen to your heart and soul and find the goodness that resides there waiting to shine through. You, the one that can't even look into your own face in the mirror, you, the one that fears fear itself, that hides behind those words of ugliness to make yourself feel bigger than God himself. No! God would never mistreat his people or loved ones the way you have mistreated your loved ones and friends. He that sits at the right hand of your father who shines his love upon you and glorifies his right as your savior, looks upon you now with sorrow for what you have become and what you have instilled upon the heads of others.

Stand tall and please don't fall, for your time, here is very precious, for you can grow, and you can receive what it is you long for, the love and unity of understanding.

Does this belong in the book? I feel like I have just stepped off the pulpit.

Child some things are meant to be said, and others are meant to be kept quiet and this lines up with the first. We needed to say what others needed to hear without yelling and thumping but with words from the heart. Kindness works better. Some just need to think about their lives and the way they live them. All children are God's children, and they deserve the very best for and of themselves. They only have to learn the values of life and the goodness of participating in it to see changes accrue before their very eyes.

You know I never know what to expect or what is going to be flowing out of my finger tips every day. Sometimes it even scares me to participate in this, yet I am always thrilled with the outcome of such beautiful words. Knowing they are not mine and how they find their way into me and out of me is just so confusing to me as a person, yet I understand the concept of energy and the connection with God but the confusion always goes back to my human self. This is me, and these words are not mine. As my husband would say when he reads page after page, WOW! I guess that sums it up. Thanks for the wow and allowing me to be part of this wonderful experience.

Child as you sit and write we give to you what it is that needs to be heard. You still procrastinate every single day yet we still come to you for it is you that must write these words as it is for others to write their words. For you see we work well with different people, just as we connect differently with other people. As I work with you, there is another working with someone else. If we get enough material out there into the people's hands, they will see it for what it is. Truth- they will start to respond to it as truth and they will feel it as truth and before you know it they will speak it and live it as truth. And if the truth be told it sure makes for a beautiful life of understanding and love.

Chapter 6

Respecting Self

As it is right now few know the difference between respect for thyself and treating thyself respectful. We know it sounds the same, but it is not.

What is the difference?

The difference is as plain to see as looking into the mirror. Respect comes in many forms and as a child of God, people all people should treat you with respect. In life, people forget to treat others with respect because they are too busy with living their own life. They tend to be in such a hurry that they walk and talk over others and very seldom give the time of day or thought to other's feelings, or to whom they are and what it is they want out of life. Do they forget they are not alone in this world of dependency? Those others feel just as greatly as they do if not more. Do they not hear the cries of confusion and disharmony in this world of yours? Do they forget that these same people have lives too, and that they may need some respect thrown their way? Yes respect is something that gets very little attention.

In the days of yonder children always respected their elders. They were taught never talk back to an adult, especially a parent. Respect sometimes came out of fear, but if you are going to use fear, this is one time it is of good communion. Now we look around and children not only speak back but with such words of hatred. They do not listen, and they have no respect for others or themselves. This we know for if you had respected you would never treat or speak to someone in this manner, whether you were taught to respect or not.

This is really a sore subject in our society today. Our children have no respect for their elders, and this makes so many of us sad. How do we teach them in today's world?

The same way they were taught in yesterday's world. Respect comes from the home and the respect, they were shown to them. To respect someone else you must also respect yourself. This is where the problem lies. Once again, we say unto you this world of yours is moving so fast the children cannot keep up, and they feel misplaced and mistreated. School is harder and faster than ever. The journey is gone the fun has disappeared. Kindergarten was a day of learning to play with your friends and to learn to communicate and share of your time. Now you have to know how to write your name before you can even go to school. The teachers bless their souls; have forgotten how to teach; now they just try to control the classroom with all the problems that have been thrown at them.

The pleasures of school and growth have been replaced with sex education. Have they forgotten how to teach this at home? Where are the parents to these children? Where is the respect for their child's life? Where is the respect of life itself?

There is a time and place for everything, we all agree on this yet no one is taking the time to see it through. Children are afraid to go to school for the fear of being shot or attacked by hoodlums and drugs. Nevertheless, they are just as determined to go to school to learn. They want a better future, and they do not want to be left behind. Now, that is respect for you. However, should they have to fight to be able to attend school? Should they be afraid every step of the way? These are your children. This is your life. This is your world that you are allowing to turn on itself without so much as a fight.

Who is going to stop this attack on your children if not you? Any mother who has a child knows full well that if her child is hurt, she becomes a wild woman to protect her young. Why can't you bring yourself to that very same attitude for all the mother's children of the world? If every mother stood tall *for all the children everywhere we would see a massive change in this society of yours. If every mother protected and loved all the children near and far your world would swell with gratitude from every mother everywhere that can't be there for their child, but will be there for yours in their time of need. What is needed is constant caring and loving of the children? Respect comes from within. Why not teach that now before it is too late.*

Chapter 7

Let The Light Shine

It is time to let the light shine in and about yourself and all others. God sends his special messengers out to his flock daily yet few people see them or hear them. He tends his flock with seedlings and new growth because the old is getting discarded daily. He worries about the outcome that he has little control over. He takes the blame for all the bad that happens to this world yet few give him thanks for the good. Even so, he never complains about his flock. He knows there is good in all, and he believes they will return to him one day knowing full well it may be too late, for all the destruction they have accrued. There is a sadness that lies heavily on this world, one that you need to break through. When one person can say something good, there is always another to take them down. Why is that? Are they afraid of good? Do they not know that they also are entitled to receive good?

Some believe that good is for only a few and bad is for all the rest of them. How foolish of those who believe in such a way. Good is there within reach for all that take the time and effort to receive. The stipulation is that you must feel worthy to receive and here lies the problem. So many people complain that life is not fair. We know this to be the truth, yet what is fair? The dictionary states: not stormy or cloudy, just or honest, conforming to the rules, open to legitimate pursuit or attack, adequate-fairness. Fair has many definitions. How many of you are following through within reason of fairness? How can you say it is not fair when you do not participate, when you run for cover all the time, or just plain run away or complain?

Now the time has come for all good people to gather and rescue themselves for all eternity.

Set the rules that all can follow easily and without confrontation upon their heads. What we mean by this is that the time has arisen to step up to the plate and start taking some swings, and if you strike out you know two things 1 that you tried, and 2. You will have another chance to try again.

That is all we ask of you. Like in baseball the family

game at one time, step up to the plate and swing. But unlike the players on the team that really want it to work, they are always looking for a home run, not a strikeout. They did not run away or complain. They got back up there and did it over and over again, and before you knew it they would swing and that bat would connect with the ball while they watched it fly out into the field knowing that they have just succeeded in their most precious moment of life. A home run to be cheered on with excitement, and possibilities of the next time up.

This is what you need to see in your future, not only see but know, without a shadow of a doubt, that you are there among the hitters not the losers. The winners of the most precious moments of life and of all eternity.

Why you ask? Some need to see it to follow it. All need a teacher who they can look up to, to follow directions to know the way. That is why there are so many rules out in your society. Rules that hold many back from becoming or being the best that one can be. With those rules comes bafflement and bewilderment of self. One of the statements or so called rule is that you are not worthy of becoming or being the head ruler of your society. You are not valued in your worth. Your equivalent of self is not worthy. You have been brain washed into accepting their words of discouragement, unhappiness, not accepting what could and should be yours, right along with everyone else.

What could and should is not to be, how can it be when you yourself know you are not worthy of such a right when there are so many wrongs? Do you think right now at this very moment in time that you are more important to someone else then you are to yourself? Think about this for a moment now. Really think here because this is an important issue, and you know you all have issues of some sort or another. Not to be lite on this subject, let's shine some light on it and really devour what this is all about.

Think of yourself as someone who is just about to sink his teeth into a big juicy piece of steak. Your thought is that it is yours, and you want it, end of discussion, you're hungry! What about the others? Aren't they just as hungry? Are you not going to share? They can get their own you say, you deserve this as you pound your fist onto the table.. But they will go hungry without. Doesn't this bother you, we ask? Don't you feel guilty? We wait patiently for the answer, and still we wait and wait and wait.

In your society only the strong survive. That is a quote we have heard over and over again, so does that make you a weakling? We think not because in every person of every gender of every nationality is an individual of oneself, their divine self, of love and understanding of a spirit, clearly evident that one has to go deep within oneself to bring forth their true identity.

To survive in this world of yours one must find this wholeness to bring forth into the light, what is right for them and others alike? You have heard it many times over, step into the light. Well, we say unto you step into your light and bring it forth into your society without fear and revel in the delightful knowledge of the truth and understanding that God our Father your Father has brought into your life. Do not falter and shrivel up and hide because you are afraid to stand up for yourself, do not fight with strong words thrown out there to hurt others in ugly meanings and disgrace yourself and spirit within. What we ask is that you feel this warmth of love and gratitude and step forward and walk the walk of forgiveness and true understanding of worth, prosperity, growth and love. Fulfill your desire to be able to grow and walk and speak of the love you have to share and the strength that swells up inside you like a tea kettle ready to boil and spurt forth the joy of the whistle the completeness, wholeness, sipping your cup of tea and enjoying the taste of perfection. However, the taste is not for everyone and some like it different, stronger, weaker and many not at all. What do you do with those that do not agree with your tea? The same thing you have always been told. Ask them just to try a little, they may like it, or discard it to try again. You can never make someone do something that is not to their liking until they are ready to give it a try. We believe that everyone is an equal and should be treated like an equal as long as they abide by the rules, here we go again with the rules but these rules are universal. Don't push, don't shove, hands off the precious merchandise, because everyone is a piece of God, a child of God and in all respect must be filled with love somewhere within their vessel, their body, to know the difference between right and wrong. You the child believe that love dwells within your very soul. You the child who waits will not find it until you release what ails you, from what detours you from the truth. You are a child of God, and he only bestows goodness and greatness upon his children. So if you have not found this, we bequest of you to start your search and don't quit until you find what it is your looking for. The gift is there in you as the Child, waiting to be unwrapped and finding the worthiness in all that you do and say, in every word that comes forth from your mouth until the truth of giving, sharing, becomes part of you as you are part of it. All are equal in God's eyes, always and forever, from beginning to end.

We gather our children together to search out the differences in all eternity. We beseech you, we hold out our hands to you. We ask you to join hands in unity and bring forth all the joy, love and harmony that one can instill in thyself. Find the peace that you have been longing for. Locate the laughter and place a hand upon your sister and brother and extend to them what you yourself would like in your life. The harmony of this planet is in your hands, and if you extend them to your fellow neighbors and reach out as far and wide as you can the link cannot and will not be broken for all time.

As I read these words, they do something to me, I get this funny feeling of longing. I'm not afraid any longer because these words, their words, have found this place inside of me that makes me think that life is possible without fear. I long to be there yet I just can't quite figure out how to do it, how do I make it happen?

The same ways you make everything else happen, one step at a time. This will not be an overnight change. You go to bed one night and wake up the next and walla. Everything is

bright and new and just like magic it has come about. No...
this is a little more complicated. It will take a little more time,
and all must gather to build God's house. If you were to start
building by yourself, you would eventually get it done but not
in the time or perfection you want or need, but if you had other
hands and bodies coming together with the skills that are
needed you would finish it much sooner, and you would
complement each other with your skills of trade for a house well
built. Have a home worthy of God's children to gather in or to
live in or to play in and to love in. A home, not a house, where
one could and should gather their children in their arms to
communicate and share with them what God expects out of
each and everyone a small four-letter word called Love. How
hard can that be?

Everyone and everything around you

is your teacher.

By Ken Keyes

Chapter 8

The Store/Complaint Department

I think back in time when I owned a little Spiritual store how grateful I was for new beginnings. This was a complete surprise that had come about. I, Kathy, was the owner of a store. I knew nothing of this business. I just knew God had called me to open this store. There were some amazing steps along the way, and I came to realize that my destiny was not in the store but in the people that walked through the doors. At first, I did not think I was qualified for the drama or the compassion of what needed to be done. I felt like God put me in this place, for people to have a place to come in order to complain. I felt like I was the complaint department at the local hangout. The things I saw and heard made me just shake my head. I was a witness to so much haphazardness and muck. The one thing I did learn was, people will be people. However, there were all kinds of people, the complainers, the loud and obnoxious ones, and the ones with true heart. I soon found that I did not have time for the first two, and they were coming in by the truck loads. As soon as they realized I no longer had time for their garbage, they eventually took it somewhere else. Thank you God. I did not miss it for a moment. At first, I tried to help them but soon realized they needed to complain and hurt in order for them to be in their comfort zone. Wow… what a way to live. Misery every step of the way, and if they did not have it, they found it or made it happen so they could always be in the center of commotion. I soon felt sorry for them but not in the way they wanted. I felt bad that they took up so much of their lives living in misery when they could have been so productive living in a healthy loving relationship. I soon learned I could not change this, that they were the only ones that could make the changes happen when and if they wanted. I soon found out that most did not want to change.

That is really when I felt the sadness seep into my soul. Who would like to live like that I would ask myself over and over again, not understanding because I hurt for them and wanted them to help themselves? When I realized I hurt more than they did I knew it was time to look in another direction. That's when the ones with the true heart came through. They are the ones that wanted to change, that wanted to grow. They wanted to connect to their very soul. They searched and prayed for forgiveness and a new beginning and were strong enough to carry it through no matter how hard it was. They had faith maybe not in themselves but in their God. They had faith that he would see them through.

I watched the ones walking through broken marriages to come out whole once again, some to find the perfect partner to share in their lives, others to grow stronger to be able to stand up for themselves for the first but not the last time and to know they are someone special. To witness others find for themselves love, how wonderful it felt to watch as they were growing, so rewarding in itself. I have seen heartache, which feels so devastating in life. I have seen mothers, and fathers come to me that have lost children in various ways. Loss is a loss, and death is death. A loss, or a death can destroy a family in more ways than one. Many say a parent should never out-live a child, and they mean well by their words, but you cannot stop the process of loss or death. It happens and I have seen the heartache that follows, the hurt and the pain you think will never be over because the love was so deep, is still so deep, that you have no idea how to get through it or around it. Learning how to live once again is almost unimaginable, and for many undesirable. I have watched and helped others find their faith in life again through the connection with their child. I have shown them that their child is not lost to them forever. They can still connect, and the knowing has helped them to go on living the best way they know how. The experience of knowing that their child is not totally gone is a gift God has given to so many if they just accept his gracious gift and see it for what it is, total acceptance of life. Here on earth and in Spirit, we can connect and do connect with our loved ones.

There was a time in my life that I was terrified of dying. I was only a teen, and I thought about death all the time. I was a sickly child, and I thought death was always knocking at my door. I was born with spirit all around me and the fear of dying was so very real to me. At the time, I knew nothing about Spirit but that they surrounded my life. I did not like what I felt or saw or heard. I didn't understand what was happening to me, and I knew nothing about controlling how I felt or asking for good. I only felt bad and knew when something awful was going to happen. I was in total denial that anything good could happen. I remember asking and praying for God to help me because I thought I was going crazy. I was afraid to have a drawer opened or a closet door opened. I had to check under the bed and keep that night light on all night long. I remember getting up in the middle of the night to use the bath room and running back to bed as fast as I could, looking nowhere but straight ahead, jumping in bed, pulling the blankets up and around me, eyes closed, and listening to my heart beat through my chest, louder and louder, all the while praying that sleep would find me quickly. Nights were hard on me and how I survived them, I will never know. I didn't share this with anyone because who would believe me? It was just childish fright or was it? As an adult I still slept with a night light on for many years until I came to realize that Spirit was around me to help me grow, not to harm me, but to help me.

Once I realized that, the fear seemed to slip further

and further away. Death was not so horrifying, and I no longer looked at death as a final punishment, fearing I would find myself stuck in a casket decaying in the earth as a final destination.

Now I look upon it as a resting place for my human body to lie while my soul continues on. Awareness has seeped into my very being that I cannot truly die. I can leave my body, and let me tell you, I have been carrying this body around for such a long time and sometimes I think what a lucky person I am going to be not to have to carry it from here to there any longer.

This vessel is not a brand new slick shining new compact vehicle. No, it is an old, battered, rusty, held-together-with-bolts-type of a vehicle. It has been through the mill, yet I am not quite ready to give it up for the new and shiny one yet. I still have repairs to be made on it, and I know it is trustworthy to carry me on to my new adventures in life. Nevertheless, when my time is up I know what will be waiting for me, peace, serenity, love, harmony, the connection of oneness, to be whole once again, to connect to divine order. Just, the excitement of knowing this is worth the wait. So until then I am prepared to go on a little slower be a little wiser and help repair those in need until they find the part that's needed to make them whole once again.

We are not human beings

on a spiritual journey.

We are spiritual beings

on a human journey.

By Stephen Covey

Chapter 9

Tired of Trying, Tired of Being, Tired of Life

You know the feeling, the drugged-out, passed-out, and don't-want to-do-it-feeling?

It's the misery of self-loathing, of wanting what we can't have, because we know it is not in our planned-out life per say. What does that exactly mean "not in our planned out life?" Who planned it out anyway? Who says what we can and cannot have? Why all the woe-is-me attitude! Why is it so easy to fall into this pattern and what has happened to us that we cannot and will not fight for our lives? We want to give up. How did we become so weak, weak as a child not ready to walk yet? How did this happen and when did this happen? I want to know I really what to know when we became so weak that we are not willing to fight for ourselves and our lives for the very being of our souls

As I sit back and look around I do not necessarily like what I see. At some time in our life, we all have to be responsible for what and who we are. However, I see the same thing over and over again, where the blame is put on others, and people are labeled as if with tags. Pain, control, not sharing, hurt, anger, misery, fallen, black mood. Penalties should go out for statements such as these, for they are excuses for someone who does not wish to stand up and acknowledge who they are, where they came from.

We all have a past, but what is so interesting is that we all do not have a future because many are weak and too afraid to stand up on their own two feet, afraid of failure so why try. It is just so much easier to lay down right in the beginning and give up and lose rather than to try and possibly fail. But what one does not see is that there is beauty in trying, for that in itself is a success and living life. Unless you try you will never see the journey. It will never be attainable for you for fear of trying. The wisdom, the journey, whether attainable or not is so sweet because while journeying you will see the pattern of life just beginning. As it draws you a picture of life, it will continue to draw as long as you continue to proceed ahead. It is something like a number picture always coloring with the same colors until you get a little braver and start adding your own color until it becomes your very own picture that no one else can ever duplicate. Your very own life, your road to success, true there have been many obstacles along the way but what a journey you have been on. An experience that only you can share with those who are closest to your heart, the ones that will understand what life is meant to be or should be for the ones willing to take hold and get on board for the ride of their lives. What is fear but injustice to your soul to the very being of who you are? It plays havoc with your lives, and most of the time wins out. Why we ask? Why do we let this happen?

How can we change it and make right this whole situation? The change begins inside with want, with the belief and with courage. For anything right, is right for all, not just a few, but what one has to see is they must want what is right, and work towards making it right for themselves, before they can help others who are spreading the blame. For it is much easier to lay blame and quit than to proceed ahead, take responsibility, and begin a new and rewarding life. Few too many have not seen the way, but we are rewarded with the knowledge that many are waking to the need of fulfilling their lives and the only way to accomplish this would seem to be to start drawing your life the way you want it to be. Step by step, as slowly as you wish, but just remember to go forward without blame or criticism, only in love and self-respect will you find your way.

Peace and Love to all.

As I wrote these words, I could feel this sensation inside me feeling sick to my stomach yet the feel of little butterflies going around and around. As I read the words that were wrote I felt the truth in them and also felt ashamed of myself for not working harder on this book and neglecting the promise, I made to complete this book. There is no time limit, yet I feel the need to hurry as if they are trying to tell me something. I have almost felt like time might run out if I do not proceed full steam ahead. What pressure to be under, yet I feel obligated to proceed. However, now it is more than pressure. I want to proceed, and I want to finish this book as much for myself as for others. I also must find the way, step by step and here before me lays a step I must and will take, that leap knowing that growth will follow or should I say I will grow as I proceed forward. That is what growth is, knowing and taking the chance, going forward and never looking back. Seeing the sunshine and day break not darkness and end of the day but new beginnings with God's help all will be delivered to us. What matters is what we accept to take on. Thank you God for this awaking

Chapter 10

Where Does A Person Go From There

I don't know if I have spoken to you about my family but like so many others, family is so important. You hear the horror stories, and I could tell you some of my own but that is not what I am here for. What I would like to share with you is this. Whether you come from a broken home or a loving home, everyone, not just some but everyone regrets something that has happened in their life as they grew up. To some it may be abuse, others hard times, and yet others will tell you about their hurts. At some time in their life not all was what they wanted it to be. Whether it was big or small there is one factor, life was not as good as it should have been. You can hear the cries and feel the pain that we all carry with us through our lives. We have become unsettled and unhappy because we cannot forget or forgive what had happened to us, and we are angry and wounded. Some want revenge. Others want pity and yet others just cannot move ahead. It's like a game board something like monopoly but instead of buying up property, we are gathering all our hurts and pains and in the process, we are disillusioned with life, our life, life in general.

How do you go forward? Just like the game you roll the dice and take a chance and square by square step by step you go forward. You may not want to end up where you do, and you may not want to do what you are called to do, but like the game to proceed forward you must take the chance and try. For that is when you start to find the light that will shine upon you, and that is when you start to heal. Step by step, and yes sometimes you may end up going backwards but remember you always have another turn and with that turn comes the rewards of growth. All of us slide backwards from time to time. It's when you get up and continue forward again that you feel the pride and the reward of not letting the past turn you around again. It is in the adventure that truth will be found, and healing will begin. Life is not about the past it is about the now (present) and the future, and the future is where you need to see for sight is a beautiful thing. Remember always look ahead at the sunrise and know that your life is beginning to be awakened to yet another sunrise to repeat itself daily for the rest of your life.

Chapter 11

How Much Can One Person Take!

How much can one-person hold within them before they tremble with the want of peace? The pain that filters into each person is gathered at intervals in different momentums. Some a quiet gentle knowing and for others as if a steam engine train has just passed them on the tracks headed for all the pain and disappointment of life, with no control to steer or slow down the motion it creates in one's life. Imagine a life of such speed, and the strength of another blowing past you or plowing you down if you happen to get in its path, of something so powerful that you as only a simple human being had no control.

What God has shown us is that we as human beings are not simple by any means. We are made up of the most extensive internal wonders the universe has shuffled together. There have been no mistakes that you as the human aspect have not but accomplished on your own. When there is pain, it is but a growth of who you are and what you have put in your path to accomplish in this life. With pain comes accomplishment or failure to accomplish.

Look at it this way, You see a path ahead of you that you must walk to get to your destination. It is full of small rocks, large boulders and fallen trees. To walk this path you must cross over or remove what lies in your way. This could be hard work and very frustrating to the one that needs to walk this path. Now a decision must be made. To go forward and start your walk knowing you will get to your destination no matter what the circumstances or give up because it looks way too hard. There are those that start to walk the path to find out later that they can't give their all to this project, and they're going to find a way around it only to fall off their path. Each of you have a path. Some harder than others for this is what everyone feels, that their path is always the hardest. Yet the truth be known, all paths are laid out. in uniform reason for the one that shall walk it. You came here to grow yet you cry with betrayal of what? Fear and pain of not succeeding. How can one succeed if one does not walk the path of life? How can one succeed if all one does is complain and cry and stay stagnant in their own pain and misery? These questions are put forth to you to ponder over, to accept as truth if one wishes.

When we come to pain, there are so many other reasons for a person to always look at oneself. Your world is infested with hatred and sorrow. We feel the vibrations as they come through wave after wave. How can one survive in this atmosphere of such confusion and pain without picking up on the troublesome feelings of others? You as a person feel for others, you care about the rest of humanity along with your animals and nature. Without these things, you would stand alone in a solid world of waste. Can you picture not having beautiful trees around to look at? They are not just there for your sight of beauty, those trees have a very important job distinction.

They are there for not only the creatures of nature to be able to feed on and live with but one of the most important aspects of a tree is for breath, to oxygenize the world. For you to not have breath you would not be. Easy concept to understand yet every day we see your beautiful world being destroyed for money, selfishness, this is not sharing. This is not caring, there is no gratitude given, only destruction. Not for just one person but for all. This pain is very real.

Water is taken for granted. You as a human body you need this very substance to survive. Without it, there is no life. However, in this very day we see your drinking water becoming toxic. The very ones that need it are contaminating it with no end in sight. We look out on your earth plane and see your fish and animals being destroyed and disfigured yet we see no changes being instilled. Why is this being done? Why is this happening? Always to come up with the same conclusion, money, selfishness, not caring nor thinking about the future, only now.

Let us take those few or many and show them what the future holds for all their loved ones left behind. How will they live and for what will they live for? What kind of future are you leaving to them? The one you so selfishly took with no regards to anyone but yourself. This is pain not only to the human race but to all of nature. Without clean water there will be no hope for the future of mankind.

Mother earth as we so kindly call her, she is like a mother who furnishes all food for your plate from the soil of her lands. When you look back in-time humans had gardens in every back yard planting their vegetables and herbs. The table was always stocked with freshness. The bounty was plenty, freshness at its best. People were healthy. They gathered their food; they ate of the goodness of mother earth. Now mother earth cries, for the soil is so depleted and saturated with chemicals that race through your bodies towards destruction of organs. It is impossible to eat healthy food now without buying or growing organically, and still you worry if it is truly safe. What has happened to Mother earth or should we say what has happened to you? Not only for you, but all those who gather and still wish to gather for their families. This needs to stop before mother earth can no longer give of her food or her services.

Sickness is in a rage. Years ago, now and then someone

you knew was ill, now a day's all you have to do is look around and see sickness, it is leading the race. But where is it running to? How can it be stopped? And who will step forward and demand a change before it runs rapid in every one's life. The children cry. The mothers cry. The fathers cry. The brothers and sisters cry. We hear this on the other side, wails of pain the regret of sadness and a longing for health for love. To watch and see someone you love suffer in sickness when there is no need is a critical but necessary step in order for others to see past the pain. Where did it start? We know the answers but what we are uncertain of is. When will it end? How long must you see or experience this magnitude of pain before you step up to the plate and not allow it to happen any longer. As a person an individual, an essence of humanity, a part of God, of universal wonder, how has this come to be and how has it not ended? These are the questions that need to be answered, not tomorrow but today!

As we watch and see we are relieved to know that all has not been given up on. Those changes can be made, and some are working at this even now as these words are read. What we are not happy about is the percentage not working at righting a wrong. What will it take to get the message across? What has to happen before you as a race see what lies in front of you? Most only look one day at a time and in some respects this is a good way to live but not in this respect. Here and now, one must not only look day to day but to the future and the possibility of disaster. There could be food shortage, water shortage and the inability to change the inevitable. Now is the time to stand tall and please do not fall. For your country, and the universe of the whole world is laying in your hands and surrendering to your wisdom of understanding and truth, that each and everyone needs to reach their hand out and up to the universal power of all goodness and ask for changes to be made and follow through and make these changes happen. In other words, all things are possible, but it takes more than words. It takes action and not just one or two people, but the majority must stand up and take action to see the results that are needed at this time in your life. It may take a little work on your part but what a wonderful feeling you will have knowing that you are helping Mother earth to reestablish her goodness to all of humanity. God is always grateful to see his children respond in the harmony of goodness.

As I read the words that were written my heart cried for all that has happened to this world of ours. I am afraid of what the future will hold for my grandchildren and yours. I know I love my family and would do all that's possible to help them, so why not this? It sounds too big of a project for one person yet we are not alone. We stand tall as a nation. Why not stand tall as an individual, every one of us, and let's make a difference. You have heard the cries and seen the mess out there, so lets gather together and make a difference. I may not be here when this comes about but why should we allow it to happen even if we are not here. For our children and grand children and for their children, let's clean this place up. It is our world and we always get what we want any other time, why not this time.

Let's make a commitment to ourselves and our

families that we will help restore our world to the place it once was... healthy, clean, and well. Let's give the world back to Mother earth once again and profit from it cleanliness.

Chapter 12

Confused

Life has set me about in a whirl and a twirl. I never know if I am coming or going and that is just about one of the worst things to deal with along with the other couple hundred things in this life of mine. However, I am not alone; imagine that! Others come to me wanting me to give them answers so they know what to do and when to do it. It would make it so much easier they say if you would only tell me, then I would do it, and I would know all will be well, and that I am on the right path, no worries. Who are they kidding?! No worries! Life is about opportunities about choices, right or wrong you get to pick. If you picked wrong this time, then maybe next time you will make the right choice and if not hopefully eventually you will make the right choice and be prouder than all get-out that you finally made it. You have taken another step in this life of yours just as I have taken another step in allowing you to grow through your own decisions that is growth.

I am here to help you grow; to help you in walking your path but you as an individual must consider and ponder all life's mysteries. How lucky we are to be able to choose when so many countries do not allow this to happen. How fortunate we are as a society, a country, an individual whom we can say and do almost anything we wish. I say, "Almost" because we would not want to take or tarnish a life that is so precious. Life and this body have been given to us. Let us not forget where it has come from and where it will go to when we are done using it.

Child you have said a mouth full in just a few sentences and you say you know not of what you speak. I say on to you that all is within oneself. What he or she does or does not do is of no difference or concern to another. It just is! Even so, all must look towards the other for insurance and endurance. They are afraid to go forward on their own, afraid of mistakes, of failure, when only one is in control, it scares the individual but when they can raise a hand and say or blame another for their mistakes along the way it becomes an easier road to walk. What we would like to see and pray to see is every individual taking responsibility for them. Not in judgment calls but in practicing the willingness of adventure and establishing a foundation of one's future in planning and making the steps, one to another and succeeding in one's own future.

Whether it is right or wrong, good or bad, you must strive in order to succeed. You must be willing to take the steps and allow the mistakes to happen and be willing to make the corrections along the way while achieving your destination. While this may seem like a hard road to walk, we say onto you, what a journey you will have along the way. What a growth for your soul, for that is why you have come here. Not for the mistakes, not for the hardships, but for the growth you will receive. To become what and who you always wanted to be, through thick and thin you can make it that is why you are here now at this time in your life.

Proceed forward and do not look back child, only look forward to the wonderful adventure of life and all it has to share with you. Congratulations on sharing this adventure with us and know that we as your helpers will always be here to help and guide you along the way, but you as the chieftain must follow your path in the best way you know how while taking full responsibility for it. This is just one step but a mighty big one. After that you will be ready for whatever is handed to you. God Speed Child, God Speed, to the good life.

The good life, we are all in search of that. Some of us think we will never see it. Others are there as we speak, or at least we think they are. This is food for thought.

Don't think of God in terms of form,

because forms are limited

and God is unlimited

by C.S. Lewis

Chapter 13

The Time Has Come

The time has come for all to receive. How, you wonder, where, you wonder, and when will this be? For all those who ask and those who walk the path in the knowledge of understanding the words of your Father, understand he is gracious with his Love and communicates daily in his need to be understood. You as the person receiving, you as the receiver must learn what his words mean when he comes forth to stand by you in his glory of understanding your most private *thoughts of awareness.*

He comes to you his child that you may receive his goodness, and he stands by you daily, that you may become aware of his attention for you as his child. He watches you and gives to you his love and understanding, that you may filter this into your own life of goodness and receive what he so graciously gives of his heart. Money may buy you things, but his love will definitely see you through to receive what it is you need, and that does not take money. When all is said and done, money does not buy all things. Some are given freely of their own choice.

Do you understand what it is we are trying to relay to you? What it is we are here to teach you? Do you understand that God your Father is available to you FREE of charge with no strings attached? Are you aware that nothing in life is free they say? Well, we are here to tell you differently. For freedom of speech has always been, and now has gone to the extent of taking the freedom from your children while not allowing them to use the word God in school. To say the pledge of allegiance, that which brings a strong community of understanding with the words being said aloud in unison of voices to allow the world to hear, as they become one voice under God, indivisible with liberty and justice for all.

What is wrong with this world where a child, a person cannot say what is in their heart? If there is a person that wishes not to participate, then let him or her withhold of their voice but to take it away from all to make a few happy, hurts and pains me to no end. This is what you call freedom of speech. What about the ones who are not allowed to speak their words of freedom? We have watched your world turn itself upside down, inside out and backwards again, and we shake our heads and hold our hearts to see what a mess you have created. It is like taking a beautiful world and creating a mud pie. People sure get dirty while trying to stay clean. Freedom means just that! We have the freedom to do and say what the heart needs to hear while not hurting another. You as an individual should be able to say the words' God, Love, Understanding, Freedom, and share it with whomever is in need. From my heart to yours, please hear the words and always know that without Love, there is no life worth living. So please love thyself as I love you, from my heart to yours child.

WOW... when I read these words, I started to feel over whelmed. I wanted to cry for all of us. I keep asking myself what is happening here, just what is going on that we can't, are not allowed to bring God up in our schools. I have taught spiritual classes at schools and have been told not to use the word God. To me that is impossible because I believe. What do I believe? I believe through God we are awakened into his spirit. We are part of him as he is part of us. How can you teach a spiritual class without bringing out his name? Impossible, so some rules are meant to be broken. This is one. I do not break rules as a habit and I am not one to preach the word of God, but I am one that believes in truth! My truth is, I believe in God and the universal power of all good. I always tell everyone I will not talk about politics or religion because that is the fastest way to a full-blown argument. What I will say is this, if you believe in GOD and LOVE that's all you need. The world would be a peaceful and loving place. No need for fighting about whose God is better than your God. That is not what he had in mind when he gave us life. What he wanted was for everyone to be blessed in his light and love, A community of PEACE and HARMONY.

I can't understand the fighting going on, the killings happening, the loss of life, the pain and hurt, families never seeing their loved ones ever again. The bombing, the loss of limbs, lives, all of mankind fighting; WHY Is this what he wanted? For what, to say your God is better than mine? To say your God is the real God. Do you really think he wanted all these deaths and hurts in his name? I am but a speck on this earth plane. If only one person hears as I hear or see as I see they will know without a shadow of a doubt that God is all good. He loves you, as he loves me. There is no difference between you and me when it comes to his love. He worships all in the same way, why can't we?! Why is this so hard to see, to believe? I feel it is the power of man and ego that interferes and destroys all that lies in its path. Is this what mankind has come to?

I say unto you child your words have been heard, and we are in agreement. Your mankind needs to make changes NOW not tomorrow but NOW. If each and everyone reached out a hand to shake, it would be grabbed. If others reached out their arms for a hug, it would be received. A kind word, it would be heard. A smile only returns. This is what God has taught you to be loving to all mankind whether big or small. God has taught you to know the difference of right and wrong and not be swallowed up in the do's and don'ts and whatever's of life. That is just too confusing, and that's when the problems start. Feel the Love as it flows through your body and extend it to your fellow man; this is what God wants for you.

Only you can make it happen. When someone says you cannot say God's name out loud don't get mad, just smile and know you have the freedom to say his name as much and as loud as you like. Sticks and stones can break my bones but names can never hurt me. Freedom is the wonderment of life.

I remember that saying from childhood. It's been a long time since I've heard it. It takes me back to the days of name calling. How insensitive a child is to another. How words can hurt so deeply. Yet it is something that even as an adult one does not grow out of. When will we all realize how much, we hurt each other by the words that escapes are mouths? How often does someone hear... you're really dumb, dummy, how stupid can you be, You'll never grow up to be anything, You're not smart enough, when are you ever going to grow up, I hate you, you're mean, you're ugly, you're fat, queer, fag, witch, what a bitch, hog, you stink, you make me crazy, are you crazy, or maybe the good old I wish I never had you or I wish you were dead. What kind of words are these anyway? Nothing any of us would want to hear. Nevertheless, they are said daily to many people, children and adults alike. Why? You know what I say, If you can't say anything nice about the person, then don't say anything at all.

What right do we have to make someone else suffer? Words hurt and are carried on forever to be remembered with pain. Some people could care less about others. Some really take offense and feel the vibration of the words. They were meant to hurt, and they have succeeded. So I guess you need to say the rhyme for it to work. We have something to throw back at them without falling into the pattern they have set. But as an adult I don't think, I can yell back (sticks and stones can break my bones but words will never hurt me) But... I can think them.

Chapter 14

Kids there is something to be said about them!

They are the most remarkable resistant human that God has put on this earth. They have the power to control from the moment their little mouths open up. Their first breath is almost simultaneous with their first cry into this world. They cry for the understanding of life, and the acceptance of all that is immortal to the birth of creation. With their first breath to their last breath, many things happen in the life of a child. They come from the father to return to the father but while they are here they are learning from their first moment of time. A journey, not any two are the same. What can be a beautiful journey for one can be a troublesome journey for another? Nevertheless, it is a journey of a lifetime never to be repeated again.

Children are invincible they say, yet time and time again I have seen real destruction flow through their troubled lives to affect them for all-time. Not knowing how to believe in a world where no hurt or harm will come to them. Always hiding and never trusting what lies ahead of them. They are troubled and confused, hurt and lonely, mentally disabled and generally hiding from themselves right along with others.

Why does this happen to an innocent we ask? Who are we to blame?

If there was blame, it would go to mankind and the lack of family unity. Everywhere, we look, and we have searched high and low and have seen a pattern which if it is not change. A destruction of sorts will accrue and has accrued in this life time. One of uncertainty, unfamiliar with the human touch, a coldness has escaped into this lifetime of yours. Time has moved way too fast and too hard and has pushed beyond what one is capable of.

In turn children right along with mankind have turned into themselves to become the power and the influence in order to survive. What we mean by this is, people are being conditioned from outside forces to take and behave outside the circle of life as we have known it.

Can you not look around and see the children taking weapons into the schools and shooting innocent people down because they were laughed at or felt mistreated by someone? They see not what they do to others as wrong. They feel proud of wiping out what they did not like instead of finding a solution and talking about the hurt. They in return retaliate with hurt. Yet they go even further and hurt anyone and everyone because they have the power and the right, in their mind not ours. You must look past the destruction, and know this child has no harmony in his life if he can pull a trigger and wipe out the lives of his fellow students.

Every day you put the TV on you are flooded with killings and murders, shooting's cold blooded and cold-hearted mistreating of others. You allow your children to sleep with their TVs on because it is so much easier than telling them to turn it off; it is time to go to sleep now. You allow the TV to enter their minds while they sleep. Their subconscious minds take in everything that they hear while they sleep filling their precious minds with hurtful words, killing, wars, fighting, screaming, yelling anything and everything that could and would destroy a young mind let alone make them fearful of life. Everything that should not enter their minds is now full of the extent of destruction. You are fearful of what is going to happen next and put the blame on others. Yet you that lay the blame are the ones who may wake up and find it may be way too close to home. We hear it, the same thing over and over… not my child - No, never your child. Then one day you wake up and look in the mirror, and you don't like what you see.

The very same person that once said not my child has got to come to grips that it can hit anyone at anytime and anyplace. A child is precious when they are born and beautiful and so ever trusting with their lives for they have no choice. They are placed into their parent's hands as a gift. Not just for a short time but for all of life. Through the good and bad, the easy and tough times and this gift needs tending to. You were given five senses for many reasons; to see, hear, smell, touch and to taste. You need to see your child, this precious gift, as they need to see you, their loving parents. They need to hear your coos, laughter and smiles right along with your frowns and discipline. With smells comes cleanliness which every person need. Touch is one of the most important factors in growth. Those hugs, ruffling of hair, holding of hands all mean love and safety to one growing up. As far as taste is concerned, all need the good taste in their decisions or opinions of one's life. You may wonder if this is the reason you were born with the five senses. This is just one of many reasons why God has given you this great gift.

Chapter 15

At Any Given Time

At any given time in your life you are given chances to improve who you are and what you do. Now what you do at that particular time is strictly up to you as an individual. You can jump on as the train is passing through, or you can look on as a bystander at the side lines and grumble that you should have or could have, yet you did not. Then you grumble that you missed out on the adventure and start to feel sorry for yourself and get angry and madder yet. Then you start to put blame on others and situations, and of course, you have an excuse to make you feel better because that is what many of you do every day of your lives.

The reason you don't jump on the train is many. First off, you want guarantees that everything will work out. When is everything always guaranteed? You can't know when you get up in the morning that the sun will be shining and not raining. Next you want to know the outcome. How do you know you will win that lottery when you buy that ticket? You don't; you are taking a chance, why not on life? So you say to yourself, I'll just wait and see what happens; let the others jump on; let them make fools of themselves; hey, if it works out, I'll jump on. Too late... the train passed you by.

Now here is where it gets interesting, you the procrastinator, the one that thought about it yet did not take action or the one that laughed at the very thought of doing something so out of the ordinary. You the bystander the one left behind getting angrier and angrier by the moment and looking to put blame somewhere because it surely was not your fault, not jumping on when you had a chance. Someone or something had to be the blame, and if you look hard enough you will always find where the fault lies because it could never lie with you.

It is so easy to put blame elsewhere, and that's what is happening in this world you call home. Circumstances... a lot of blame have been put there. Life.... in general, you'll see a list growing there also. Family... my goodness this list of blame never seems to end only to get longer as time passes you by.

Religion… here lies a real problem; this one gives you a right to say, "I can't. It is against my religion," but is it really? How many make religion their excuse to point a finger and shake a head to judge another. Who are you to judge? Job… how you dislike what you are doing and counting the days until you no longer have to put yourselves through that horrible experience everyday of your life.

You wonder why so many of you have lost your income, your life support, the one thing that pays for the food you eat, the house you live in, clothes you wear and all your necessities. Life… is an experience, a once in a life time experience. To behave in a manner of appreciation for life and what it stands for. You the people should always be proud and happy to be. What you ask? Just to be. Be what? ALIVE!

Heaven on earth is a choice

you must make,

not a place you must find.

By Wayne Dyer

Chapter 16

You Know... You Just Know

When this became the heading, I had no idea what we were going to talk about. And as I continue to write I still do not have the faintest idea what spirit wants to say or will say so I just keep typing knowing that any minute now they will take over and give to me what it is you need to hear or maybe know. What do I know?

That's exactly right. What do you know? More than you think you know, and we will show this to you. Everyone everywhere knows something that someone else does not. Or at least they think not. It may not be something new but when it is said differently it awakens another individual to understanding something they thought they did not know when all along, they knew it to understand ourselves and our souls.

Have you ever had that aha moment when you just knew what they were going to say or go somewhere you have never been, but you knew somehow, some way. You had been there before. The phone rings and you know who is calling. Many think its funny, others think it is weird and others just know. You all know! Ever think of someone or dream of them and boom the phone rings, or they show up at your door or you just happen to bump into them in the store. Aha You just know... Dream about that someone who got in an accident or died or maybe just a terrible uncomfortable feeling that dreadful feeling that something bad is going to happen, and it does. You just know... Do you like to know these things? Not necessarily but even so you do. Can you do anything about them? Most of the time not, but sometimes you are shown or told things in order to help someone from getting in that accident or hurt in some other way. You can use these (you just know) feelings and try to improve on them. Ask questions and listen for the answers, meditate, pray for whoever needs it, including yourself, and that you may be able to help the person in need.

Develop who you are and seek out the soul, your soul. You all have them and many right now as I am writing this feel themselves awakening. Their souls are knocking on their chests saying I am here; it is time to start growing. Let's work together, let's develop, let's grow and see where it is we need to be, not just in your lives but in your spiritual journey, your awareness of oneness with your father. You the daughter, the son, stand at the right hand of your father. You his child, we ask that you seek out the awareness or self, yourself, your purpose for this life time. This journey is for you and you alone. Every journey is for growth, to become the person the entity of the moment.

Time is of the essence. Our time is so very different than your life time. Our time is one, is whole, while yours is a moment to moment always running, never to catch up when you run behind. We just are. This is something you must try. You will find this in your meditations. Time does standstill, or you can look at it as it flew by. It is all in the eye of the beholder. We would like to explain it to you like this, you remember the growing spurts you had as a child and youngster, and then when you became an adult you no longer grew in that way yet you continue to grow in other ways. Even as a child you grew in many ways other than size. You crawled, walked, talked, read. You learned to trust. You learned right from wrong, funny from sad. You even learned how to get what you wanted when you wanted it. As an adult you take yet another journey as in taking a training, going back to school, finding work, raising a family, supporting ones you love, becoming heads of households.

As your children grow up you find yourself yet on

another journey. Some find themselves completely lost because what they knew and what they did for such a long part of their life is no longer needed and they just kind of float around looking for more, looking for growth. They may not know this, yet they surely feel it vibrating in their very souls.

They may start looking for churches to go to, classes to take, spiritual books to read, and bibles to ponder through day after day. They may come across an energy class only to find out it is about healing, a speaker on meditation. How many times have we heard this one; I can never stop my mind it is always going, "maybe they can help me to calm it down," They find a development class, and find out everyone has gifts to be developed.

What, I have gifts? Yes... you have gifts. Then you make the decision to start your journey one day at a time. Some slower than others and some are so sure and want to grow so fast they jump in head first and learn to swim along the way and we are hoping they don't drown. This is a journey that is waiting for you.

We suggest you take your time and learn to do one thing at a time. Learn to do it well, then to go on to the next. Too many classes too fast will only confuse and bewilder you. You can never learn and practice like you need to in order to develop. Spirit will show you the way, but you must take the steps and proceed forward with love in your heart. This is for growth not for ego. If your ego steps in you have defeated the purpose, the purpose is to develop your gifts for your soul to grow. Ego has no place in this journey of yours.

Chapter 17

What Am I Going To Be When I Grow Up?

That is a question I always asked myself, and by the time I reached my thirties, I thought I had finally found the answer. It was so strange asking myself at such an age what I am going to be when I grow up. Aren't I grown up? I have been married, had four children, several grandchildren, and still I ask the same question. What am I going to be when I grow up? Something was wrong with me.

I just knew it, yet when I look back, I did all the things I thought I should do. I fell in love, got married, raised my family, took part in all their activities, became a young loving grandmother and went back to school searching for what was calling me. My problem was I did not know what I was searching for until I met this gentle, wonderful man who was excited about life and what it had to offer. He suggested I attend his Spiritual Development Classes. I thought about it and shrugged my shoulders. I needed to think about this for awhile. However, it was not as long as I thought. I soon called my girlfriend and asked her if she would like to go with me? Yes, she said, so the following Tues. night both a little nervous we went on our first adventure into the spiritual realm. We had no idea what we were getting ourselves into and to this day I can still feel the excitement for me and the terror for her. By the end of the evening, my girlfriend decided she could not attend again. This was just too much for her. I, on the other hand, as nervous as I was, knew without a shadow of a doubt that I would continue those classes no matter what. I had a calling. I knew I had found what I was looking for. Yet I was a little nervous about going back alone so I asked my husband Michael if he would like to join me. Don't get me wrong I would have gone back with or without him, but I knew this was going to be a long journey and I really wanted him to come along with me to share and grow together. And to this day I have never regretted asking him because now he knows what I am and respects what it is I do, without asking me a lot of foolish questions and understanding who I am.

Now back to the story, Michael came along, but

before he comes, I requested one thing of him, that he attends at least three classes before he makes his decision to quit or continue to keep going. I was really worried about the quitting. He decided he would give it a chance and after the first night, he said to me, "Honey, I don't know if I really want to go back there." This is when I said to him, "you promised you would give it three times. Anytime you do something that is new it is always strange and feels awkward. Just give it a chance." Well, after the third time he had decided he was getting something out of the class and enjoyed learning and receiving.

We were taught to give healing at the beginning of each class. Hands on healing running energy wow. The first-time Stanley our teacher came to me and told me I was going to heal someone I looked at him, shook my head and said, "I can't heal anyone." He smiled at me and shook his head and said, "Dear child you are right you are not healing anyone. You are just the instrument. God is doing the healing. You just happen to be the vessel he works though." Now said like that I was much more open and receptive to giving this a try. I was greatly delighted in the rewards that I felt. How could I an ordinary human individual lay hands-on someone and request healing?

I asked myself that many times over, and every time I did, something strange happened. I would stand behind someone requesting that I be a vessel for God's work, I would become very warm and this beautiful energy would tingle through my hands. The first few times I was nervous and a little uncomfortable but as time went on this heat would surge through me and into the person receiving the healing... I as the vessel gave... yet at the same time received... This beautiful energy that I was connecting with was coming from a universal space of time that God created for just this purpose... A laying on of hands... energy is within us and all around us to be used as a connection to flow through our bodies into those that need to be repaired or replenished. We are just starting to realize what we have within our very beings. We were always told in school that everything is energy... we all knew this, yet it never really made any sense to me until I started working with healing.

Through breath (as this is what makes us tick) and God's light. Healing occurs... Now I could get all scientific with you but those that know me know I do simple... because it does not have to be hard to learn or do. You just have to want it, practice it, maybe take a couple of classes in healing energy and do it... God works with those that seek him out...

Since the beginning of time, we have grown in a new awareness of how energy works through us and flows into those in need. Sometimes I am of the belief that if you believe, then it is so. I have become a Reiki Master and Quantum-Touch Instructor. I do healing work every week in our Meditation classes, helping others learn that they have this gift also. I have learned that energy is all around us, within us, waiting to be used.

There are many ways to connect, many ways to lay hands on, different positions, different breath work, different symbols and words to be said. However, when it comes to connecting, I have found out that if you just ask and be willing to accept and allow the energy to flow IT HAPPENS.... I am not saying, not to take a class for that is how we learn, how we feel, how we learn to trust ourselves in order to do the best job we can.... What I am saying is that we all have a gift and through classes we can learn to open these gifts much more clearly, and faster than trying to learn by ourselves.... We are seeing hospitals opening themselves to energy workers. Why you ask? Because it works....., They are seeing it with their own eyes and there is a calling for it. People are seeking it out, requesting it. Their stays are shorter. Their strength is stronger, and they feel the love that comes with the healing energy.

The ones that receive know without a shadow of a doubt that their bodies crave this healing energy, and they know it's not the person whom is in charge. They know where this energy originates, and they open their hearts and souls to feel the energy enter their beings and grow with appreciation and wonderment and they give thanks to the Father, who so graciously sends his energy to them. We as his children are part of him as he is part of us. We belong as one. A unity as it should be.

Wow child you have said it all. We agree with you that healing energy comes from our Father. He has put this into place from the very beginning. Mankind has only worried about the energy of things versus the energy of life. Energy was discovered many life times ago, and it always comes back to the beginning as if it is brand new. Scientists have told us what energy is and how it works, but many do not like science or become bored with the subject. Just give me what I want, and I don't care how it works. You as a person create your own energy and this is what is happening in your world today.

Energy follows Energy.... Give me... give me... give me... Take.... take... take... Want... want... want... Cry... cry... cry... Demand... demand... demand... More... more... more... Complain... complain... complain... Holler... holler... holler... Anger... anger... anger... When does it STOP!

You have backed yourself as a human race into a corner and are looking for someone to get you out. And when that someone promises you the moon, you believe them, for you want out. You put your thoughts, and your energy in others promises only to see them destroyed. Now time passes, and you look back and you blame others for your mistakes because it is easier for you to put the blame on someone else. Shame on you, for you was the one that backed yourself into the corner, not someone else. No one took your hand and made you do what you did... You followed the energy of want to the point of destruction and now once again you cry to be saved.

Instead of going within and living within your means, instead of sharing, giving, helping, speaking the truth and taking control of your own energy you fell into the WANT mold. Even knowing this, you did not want to give up. You still wanted more and demanded more, even when your plate was full. Then again, you must put the blame somewhere it does not belong. This circle of energy is all around this world as we speak, doing its harm, its damage, doing what it can to destroy the harmony of unity.

As we look upon mankind, we see different things coming to a head. People losing their jobs, income they must have to survive. Food to put on their tables, clothes to cover their bodies for warmth when it is cold, for protection of oneself. People losing their homes, homes they must-have for shelter for their families, a roof over their head to call home, a place to go when one wants to reunite with family, feel protected, and family unity. People are losing their insurances, medication, and hospitalization, to stay healthy, strong. The one that hurts us most are the people losing themselves as a whole.

Families forgetting how important they are to each other, not giving time to those in need. You have forgotten how to lay a hand upon your loved ones, not by force but by a desire. LOVE is lacking, TRUST is lacking, but most of all FAITH is in short supply....

We ask you child as we ask all around you. WHEN WILL THIS STOP? We hear all of you asking this all of the time, but you are asking for the wrong reasons. You are asking because you want MORE......Not because you want family unity back, or maybe you want your family to respect and love again. Not because you want God back in your life.... No you ask out of selfishness, and as long as that is what you want you will receive what you get, and it does not look very pretty out there now does it?

The world when seen through a child's eyes

greatly resembles paradise.

By Unknown

Chapter 18

Can It Change?
How and When Will It Change?

Again we are back to the beginning. When God said to you be still and hear me. Have you stilled yourself lately? Have you given him a chance to answer your questions? Have you looked upon him for the answers you are in search of? We think not, for if you did you would know what he asks of you. Is it hard you ask? Not really any harder than all the misery you have invited into your lives. Is it fun you ask? Oh it could be

the most pleasant most rewarding thing you have ever done.

Then why don't I know what it is?

Because you have not asked, you have not prayed, you have not talked to God as he should be talked to. He is your Father. Some of you have a problem talking to your earth father so how can you possibly talk to one so great? You do not share in the communion of life. Many are jealous because they never had a father to talk to. Even so, what I say to you is that you have a Father someone who believes in you and waits for you to establish communication with him. He is saddened by the fact that you do not trust him and yet you blame him for things that happen in your life. He is not to blame for he shares in your grief. What makes you sad makes him sad. What hurts you hurts him. What he does for you is to pick up after you. He tries to read your mistakes, he tries to give you salvation, but you are the one who turns the table on him and lays blame once again as soon as the times grow tough. Instead of conversing with him and asking for his help before things get so out of hand. You wait until you have no choice, and then you CRY for help and by most standards, it is too late,

Yet your Father comes to you in your time of need and gives his love to you, sends his Angels to watch over you and sends his Spirit Guides to help you along the way. God has many helpers and this also enfolds the Earth plane where he has many Earth Angels to help those in need. His SONGS are your songs. His WORDS are your words. His LAUGHTER is your laughter, and His LOVE is your love. Develop who you are and work with what God has sent to you.

Pay attention to your dreams.

God's angels often speak directly

to our hearts when we are asleep.

By Eileen Elias Freeman

Chapter 19

Spirit

Spirit comes to you in many ways. We can actually feel Spirit

God, Our merciful Father has given all of human kind many gifts. He not only gave mankind an opportunity to better themselves; and to grow in the light, but he has provided helpers, which help you while they grow in helping themselves. What we mean by this is that God our Father has the link to all mankind along with Heaven and Earth. When you live on *earth, you are here to learn, grow, through mistakes, wisdom and understanding, along with forgiveness. They all have a part not just in this life time but many life times ago. After you have left this planet earth you depart to a place where you continue to grow to learn. The values are all the same yet very different for the individual. It is what you crave to be, whole, to be pure, to be honest, to have integrity and to have justice for all. This sounds very human, and you have heard the words before many times over. Spirit signs up for growth and with growth, he is assigned to human kind in helping them to develop themselves in ways beyond our imagination. They know that they can only do so much, and they must let their student grow in their own way. However, they are there to direct; give little pushes, hints, and help them to find their path. Others are there to communicate with them through thought patterns, energy waves, giving you permission to connect with them and learn from them in this beautiful way of understanding.*

They come in thought forms. You hear them as you hear through your ears yet very differently. Sometimes people think that this is their own thought but soon to find out, they speak differently than you do, they are more loving then you are, more forceful in their beliefs and much more determined to be heard. Many people push them away because they are afraid. Many don't have time for them, and many just are not ready to go on this route yet. Time and time again we hear, if only I would have done this earlier in my life, if only I would have listened, if only I had taken the time to learn to develop to learn how to communicate. If only, if only, it does not matter how long you wait or when you start. Spirit will always be near you and when you are ready, they will appear, to be your best friends on an exciting adventure. Now when I say appear, I mean just that, some do appear to you. You will not only feel them, you will see them, you will hear them, and you will grow in whatever ways it is best for you. Did we not say at the beginning that God your Father has gifts, many gifts for you? These are just a few of them. The rest of the gifts comes in the way of giving to others what you yourself have learned. This is probably the biggest gift your Father has given to you. To feel fulfilled, to be able to give to another without taking away from yourself. To be able to speak the words you have been given, and know they will be converted into words of harmony, peace and understanding. To be able to bring this to your world that is in trying times as we write, as we put together the words that they themselves must hear, must feel, must know right from wrong without someone slamming their fist on the table and saying you must do this! There is no must, there is only the want to be strong, to be proud, to be healed, to be one with God your FATHER. He has given you a choice. He welcomes you to his paradise. He gives to you only happiness. He sends his teachers to be among you to help you in your search of life. He sends to you what he does best. He sends his LOVE, his UNDERSTANDING, and he serves you a platter full of bountiful fruits that you may go on your journey and develop and search out all the good he has given to you. For he is your provider, he shelters you in his home, for you will never be alone as long as he is with you.

Talk to him, share with him, converse with him, get to know him in all his glory for he is your Father as you are his Son and Daughter. You are his Children. He treats you fairly. He shares all that he has, and he sends you all that you receive through the love of Christ Jesus.

WOW...I know I said wow, but I don't have many words after that. I am sitting here just shaking my head because as always, you put it in a form I can understand, and it has hit my heart and brought tears to my eyes because I, not only I, but we all have special gifts that God has given to us whether we are in human form or Spirit. How could anybody ask for anything else? I have come to the conclusion that we are a very lazy, selfish society that only wants and is too lazy to connect to what could rightfully be theirs with a little work. You know people go to work because they have to, complaining all the way. They do what their bosses say because they have to, only to resent their jobs and people and the unhappiness follows them. When all they have to do is reach for the gifts, and learn to listen, learn to communicate and follow what it is they are searching for.

I understand this part because I have been there right along with everyone else. Until the one-day Spirit sent a gentle man my way, and I listened to him, I went to his classes, I developed my awareness of Spirit, and I continued to learn. I got lazy along the way, and I strayed, only to come crawling back when times got too hard, and I felt all out of sorts. I needed my base, I needed to connect again to find myself. I needed what every man and women needs... PEACE. It was as plain as the look on every ones face. So many of us crave peace, we need Peace, desire Peace, within ourselves, among others and the biggest yet, WORLD PEACE. So I say to you, you can crave an even demand Peace but in order to receive Peace you must give Peace, to give Peace you must learn, to learn you must call on spirit to help you receive what is rightfully yours. Peace.

Child I could not have said it any better... Peace is craved, but it is craved out of Fear.... You cannot receive Peace without releasing fear. This is the way of the universal energy that flows through you. You as a person have a choice on what you have and how you receive it. You must connect to the positive energy that flows through you to your inner being and ask God to fill you with the right and perfect you, so you may be able to grow in the needs of others. It sounds like a lot of work but really all it is, is a connection of the right energies.

We as a Spirit speak to you, show you. Connect to us and let us help you. Come freely without demand. Ask what it is you must, and we will show you the way. The way we connect to Kathy (yes we said your name) we do prefer Child but we want them to understand what we are saying. Kathy comes to us by sitting in meditation; prayer and asking for us to come to her; so she may write. We fill her being with the want of words. The words flow out, and she does her best in writing these words down. Our energy is much stronger than hers, but she meditates to strengthen it. She has given us permission to write through her. She is the channel or vessel as we say. We give her the words. She types them out as fast as she can. We try to connect in the best way we know how. She can request slower, louder, ask questions, but mainly she inputs our words. We thank her for this in many ways but the one she mostly enjoys is the love we share with her in the learning of new wisdom. Anyone and we say anyone, is able to receive if he or she practices, meditates, and allows the energy to flow without being fearful. We cannot take over. You are the human in charge. We are the spirit guides who are blessed to teach you, to help you in your quest for Spiritual Development. You will know when your time is here, when you are ready, for you will hear your soul knocking on your chest saying now, now, now... I am ready to grow. We wait for you. We are patient. This is what we do best, and we understand. When you are ready to connect, let us know, and we will gladly show you the way.

Again, you have said so much, and of course, it is all truth. Even so, fear does stand in the way. I remember when I first started getting messages. This can't be happening to me. How can this be? I use to ask this time and time again. The same answer came over and over again. TRUST.... Again a WOW moment... I felt like a fool... What if I said the wrong thing? Giving messages was a difficult thing for me to get through until I learned the secret. I had to trust in myself knowing that Spirit would never give me anything that could hurt someone. God only works out of love. I must trust what I receive and give it in the most loving way as if God was giving the message himself. For that is who I am. I am God's child bearing his words for his other children. I always start out my message work or readings with a ritual if we must use that word. I circle myself, the room I'm in, and the building that holds us in God's white light of protection. I ask for my doorkeeper to watch over who steps in, and I call on all my guides, including their guides, to join us and I ask God to give me the words that his child needs to hear, and I always thank him in advance for allowing me to be a channel through him. Then I say the Our Father (Lord's Prayer) I feel it is the strongest most powerful, beautiful prayer, there is. It works for me. I feel myself connecting to this beautiful energy that fills my being. As I breathe deeply I feel my body consumed, and I just start talking, sharing in what I hear, see, and feel. I find most of the time all their questions have been answered before they even ask them. If they have questions, we go forward and answer them the best we can. We do not interfere where we know we are not to go. This is a personal and spiritual growth for those that come to me.

When my human side steps in, or my ego, I fail at what it is I need to do. I have to give myself up to Spirit and rely on what they give me in order to give to another. Trust was and is the word.

Child you have given a good description on what it is you do. Many do it in different ways, but as you said trust is the word. In God, we Trust…. These words have been very powerful words for the entire human race. Now there are those that wish to replace or wipe them out. You as whole or as an individual must decide to keep God in your lives as a want of justice, as a permanent fixture in this society of yours. For without God where would you be? Who would cry for you? Who would send his enlightened to you? Who would give his love unconditionally for you? Remember he wants nothing in return but for you to love yourself as you love your neighbor. He freely gives of his words, his love, and he trusts you with all his heart knowing that you are his child and he is your father and as your father, he looks out for you and wants only the best for you his child. Go in peace my child... Go in peace

Chapter 20

I Am Scared

We need God in our lives.... We need his protection and his love... how can a few rule over so many? What is happening to our society when you can't say God out loud or the pledge of allegiance in the schools? When they take it off our money; when we can't sing it before a ball game; when the coach can't pray before a game. God was brought into our lives for a reason. He has been a part of our lives for as long as any of us can remember. He is an important part of who we are as a person, a family, a group or a religion. We call on him for weddings, uniting who we are as a couple. We call on him for funerals, when we ask him to show our loved ones the way home. We call on him for our losses, to help us out of despair. We call on him when we have no one else to call on. We ask his forgiveness knowing we will get it. He comforts us. He gives to us. We are a better person, better society with him in our lives. So why are we turning our backs on him and allowing someone to take him away from us? I just don't understand and I am fearful of what will happen to all of us without him in our lives.

As you should be child. Without your Father in your lives, it will no longer be a family or community of love. Tension will rise. Blame will be put out into the ethers but there will be no one to answer when the help sign goes on. For you will stand alone in a cold unpredictable world of hardness and crime.

Chapter 21

Children and Prayer

I have to share this with you because it happened only a few weeks ago and I was so disturbed by what I saw. My husband and I went to a funeral, we were at the cemetery, and the minister asked everyone to gather closer to the casket, and he led them in the Lord's Prayer. We were at the back of the room, and as we moved up and started praying I saw something that scared me. I usually pray with my eyes closed but spirit wanted me to open my eyes and what I saw unnerved me. I saw all the young adults and teenagers looking around feeling nervous and not knowing what to do. You see. They did not know the prayer. They did not know how to pray. They were looking at each other shrugging their shoulders playing with their cell phones. What has happened to family unity and teaching your children how to pray? Kids must learn and they must learn how through their parents, family, church. They need a base, a solid foundation if they are ever to grow in a spiritual way.

Even as I write this, I must tell you when I am doing a session with someone, and I ask them if they know the prayer "Our Father" they look at me, and I have to tell them it's ok I will give them the prayer. I have given the prayer to quite a few people, and I ask them to use it as if it is a gift. When they want to talk to God be sure to say the prayer and wait for the answer. He will be sure to make contact. Just like the telephone rings and you answer. However, when he rings you must also answer. This I know through Spirit. Thank you Father.

Once again, you have shared something with us that gives food for thought. Children do need a foundation as they start out. This you see in school, work and play. They also need one in communion and conversing with God. Bed time prayers were once the answer, Church or temple was another, community, togetherness. Children did not always like it, but they did it. They learned who God was in their own religion. They learned prayers and how to say them. As adults they then made choices of what they practiced and where they went, how they wished to pray, if they wished to pray. Nevertheless, they had the foundation and as anything else. That is the best way to start, solid and secure for growth to follow.

We look forward to the time when the power

of love will replace the love of power.

Then will our world know

the blessings of peace.

By William Ellery Channing

Chapter 22

Trying Times

When I had my little Spiritual Store people would walk into the store in search of many things. Some wanted to buy gifts for a loved one; maybe an Angel or a beautiful statue. Others would come into the store looking for something to heal themselves with. It could have been a special healing stone, or a rosary. Some came to get learning tools such as a deck of Angel Cards, Rune Stones, a book on development and others came for Meditation

Classes, Development Classes. The ones that really stood out are the people that came in for help whether it is for them or loved ones. They came, and they came by the bushel full. Sometimes I got so overwhelmed with what Spirit sent to me that I would call on them and ask them why are you sending these people to me? I am only a human being, there is no way I can help them, this I was sure of. They said to me Child be aware of what it is you say for we would not send them to you if you could not help them. How? I would say, and they would tell me to just be in the moment. Be still, and listen... Each and everyone came for a reason, some way beyond anything I could have imagined. I had a person we will call her Mary walked through my door one day, and she was looking around and around and I asked her if I could help her, but she said she was only looking. I told her to take her time, and if she needed anything to let me know. It wasn't unusual for people to walk around the store several times and check everything out. We use to have a saying. You have to go around the store at least three times before you see everything, and then you still missed a lot. It wasn't long before I noticed she was no longer walking but pacing and pacing, and once again, I asked her if I could help her but I asked her in a very different way. I said to her what can I do for you? She got very agitated and started telling me a story about her life, and as she told me, she started pulling her sleeves up on her arms and I was staring at ugly red welts, cuts, red, raw. There were so many cut up and down her arms. She was a grown woman with heart ache. She was in a very difficult spot, needing more help then I could give her. However, I remembered what Spirit had told me, they walk through your door for a reason. So I opened up to Spirit and asked them for help with this situation, because I did not want a situation happening in my store.

As the story unfolded, she was wanted by the police and all this poor woman wanted, was to see her children and to let them know how much she loved them. When she showed me her arms, I asked her WHY? Why would you do that to yourself? Her answer just blew me away. She said to me, it is the only way I can stop the pain. By inflicting pain to herself, she was stopping the pain in her heart. It never lasted long enough so she had to continue to hurt herself for what she had done. I did not understand it, but I felt the pain that she was in and knew for her sake the only way she could or would get help would be to turn herself in and get the help; she needed to repair her life. She had to take the steps herself without them coming after her and arresting her. She found her answers as we talked; she found what she had been searching for. I saw the look on her face as if peace had made its way through to her. It did not come in a box or off the shelf, it came through Spirit.

Spirit sent her to the store where she could hear the words she needed to hear in order for her to make some decisions in her life. When she left, I just about crumbled. I was devastated to see so much pain and so much love all at once in a woman that could not find her way. I was relieved when she walked out the door, knowing Spirit works in miraculous ways, thanking God for all his help and asking him to please watch over her. I never saw Mary again, but I knew that whatever happened, it was in her hands now. At first, I thought she was brought to me just for help, but I soon learned the truth for what it was. It wasn't long after my experience with Mary that cutting became a big thing in children's lives... many close to me and parents coming to me sharing the same problem that they are having with their children. Cutting... it was like a big epidemic in children's lives and still was... the thing to do. You could find it in the computer on how to cut; you could join cutting groups, how sick was this. You know I learned something from Mary, I remember she said she was in pain.

So I looked around at all these children, and I wondered how much pain they were in emotionally. They had a way to express their pain without talking about it. As sad as it is, truth be told, our children are in a rare form these days. They are crying out for help, all they want is the love that they deserve. I know there are the few that cut just to be in the group or to be different, but the majority has a problem, and the problem cannot be fixed if there is no communication between the families. Remember, when God placed that beautiful infant in your arms, how vulnerable he or she was, and you just knew at that moment that God had given you the best gift you could ever receive. What happen to your beautiful child? Nothing, they're still there... ARE YOU?

Child what you experienced in your daily life brings you that much closer to the people you can help. You took things on in this lifetime of yours so you would be available to help those in need. Much you have experienced through your own life, and the rest comes to you when it is needed. There was a time when you thought you had to experience it all in order to help those in need, so you could say to them, I know how you feel because I have been there, or I was there once myself. This puts you in the driver's seat as far as giving them the opportunity to open up and share their darkest secrets and fears. You have helped many in this way but what we say to you now is that you no longer have to experience the situation to be able to help. We can send those that need help to you and while at the same time you are helping them, they are teaching you. Always, you are the student while being the teacher. You had to go through some of it because you requested it before you made the journey to this earth plane, knowing the experience would help you on your journey in your healing work. However, that is no longer the case. Now you are wiser, with much wisdom and knowledge, and through our eyes, we will help you to achieve.

Thank you, it sure feels good to know the past is done, and I can move forward without the heart aches knocking me down every time I turn around.

Your beliefs become your thoughts.

Your thoughts become your words.

Your words become your actions.

Your actions become your habits.

Your habits become your values.

Your values become your destiny.

By Unknown

Chapter 23

There is a Story to be Told

She has a-real story, one of the heart and soul and one of pure love, a mother's love for her child. A helplessness that takes control of her life when the child falls ill, and she feels there is nothing she can do. She had the fear of losing her child and the strength to look further than her doctors when they fail to have answers.

There is pride and ego involved. There is a drive to believe your child will get through this somehow, yet puzzled to find the way. There is a knowingness of power, yet not in the doctors for they have failed, went through all the tests, drugs and guessing games. The names of diseases they throw at us and treated, only to find no answers. Yet we are still in search of what? We are in search of knowing the feeling we have buried inside of us for our children's protection, we were put here to protect our children. To help our children grow to be honest, reliable, ambitious, loving, radiant beings. From the moment, they were put into our arms; they became a part of us. We became a part of them. Connected soul to soul, Spirit to Spirit, we have come together to grow step by step.

As a mother I love my children. Every breath I took as a mother was for them. Every fear that arose was for them. I am sure I had instilled fear into them from day one. I feared how much to dress them, not too cold, not too hot, how to lay them in a crib, so they don't choke, sneaking into their bedroom several times a night just to lay a hand upon their little bodies to make sure they are still breathing. The thought of losing my child something so precious, would put a weight on my chest that would not lift. Even as my child grows the same weight lies upon my chest. The fear we mothers go through. Don't cross the street you could get hit by a car, don't talk to strangers they might kidnap you, don't eat to much sugar you'll get sick. Hold my hand in the parking lot or the cars will run you down, Keep your hat on your head, or you'll get a cold, wash your hands, and wipe your nose. All good mothers go through this. I knew I was not alone. Fear Yes? But Truth in what we believed. We coach them as they grow; we instill virtues as they grow, right from wrong, and good with bad. And yes we put the fear of God in them. We instill fears in our children for loves sake. This fear they grow up with. It was not our intention for them to be fearful. All we wanted was for them to be careful. Such a difference, yet the way we have done it and still do it continues to cause fear, which causes pain within the Spirit of the child, for even as we grow and as grownups, we still hold on to all the fears that were thrown at us in our youthful years.

I saw the angel in the marble and

I carved until I set him free.

By Michaelangelo

Chapter 24

Nightmares / Night Terrors

People all have problems of some kind or another and try to work them out the best they can but when it comes to their child, many parents are beside themselves when they do not know how to help them. They try the professional route only to find their children drugged up with medication, and the problem not solved. Then they start looking elsewhere. This is when they find me. Someone will come to me and tell me that their child is dreaming or having nightmares, and they can't wake them up! They get hysterical because this is happening all the time. They are fearful, and they are tired because of the lack of sleep. The children don't want to go to bed, and the parents are afraid for them because they don't know what will happen to them when they do go to sleep. They have no way of controlling what is going on in their child's life. They have no way of fixing what is wrong when they don't or can't understand it themselves.

When the child has the nightmare and starts screaming the parent wakes the child to find them still screaming or crying with, wild, glassy eyes that look right through them as they are calling them by name. They're not there. You can't wake them. Some children walk around the house searching and searching for what we do not know. Some call out your name, mommy, mommy and you're holding your child and talking to them while you're rocking them, and still they can't see you. It is one of the scariest moments of a parent's life. Why? Because it does not end, it only gets worse.

I know, I have been there with my own child. Every story is a little different but all very much the same. I'd like to share my story with you. It was many years ago when my child was about eight years old. She was my oldest child, sweet as could be, never giving me an ounce of heartache. I was not into the Spiritual life like I am now, but I did know about God. I was soon to find out what Spirit had in store for me through my child. First I must say that my daughter was not sleeping well. Dreams, headaches followed, and then the nightmares started, Night terrors which were terrifying for both of us. Then the loss of weight (she was so thin already, this, she did not need) I took her to a Dr. and he suggested medication. This did not help. The nightmares became worse. This is how it began... Every night she went to bed, she would dream...she would wake up screaming, terrified, she would run from her room down the stairs through the house into my bedroom and throw herself on top of me, and this is how I woke up every night for several weeks. What was so unusual about her story is that each night it continued. It would start out the same way and always add something on at the end. Now imagine a child any child going through this. Her dream starts out with us, her parents leaving the house. She was left to baby sit her two younger sisters (she did not baby sit yet) as soon as we pulled off in our car a black car pulled up. A bald man dressed in black with dark glasses came up to the house knocked on the door and would call my daughter's name out and ask her to open the door and let him in. (I use to work midnights and when I laid down to rest the girls knew they were never to open the door to a stranger, (one of our biggest rules in the house). So of course this scared her. She would hide behind a half wall in our home by the door and would not let him in. As the nights progressed, he came every night and the dream continued to threaten her. It always started out the same, and each night would add another facet. He would pound harder; threaten her to open the door. She called her best friend and her father came over to our house, and this man killed her friend's father. Now my daughter has guilt that her best friend's father is dead. She was scared, terrified but would not open the door. Then she called the neighbor next door, and he killed the neighbor. My daughter was beside herself not wanting to go to sleep at night afraid of what would happen next. Then the man in black opened up our mail box that was a shoot into our home and looked at my daughter and told her if she did not let him in, he would kill her parents!

By now, my daughter and I were beside ourselves not knowing what to do. Her headaches were getting worse, and her weight loss was worrying me. I did the only thing I knew to do. I prayed to God to help us. I was scared for my daughter, and I did not know how to stop this.

I also did the second thing I knew to do. I took her to the doctor again. I told him about her nightmares, and he looked at me like I was a crazy person and asked me what I thought those nightmares were going to do to her, would they harm her? I said yes they already were. I was afraid for my daughter, I was afraid the nightmares were going to destroy her. He laughed. I lost all control. I could not help her, so I was putting her in someone else's hand who is supposed to help her. Someone who is supposed to be a healer? He was more concerned with her weight loss and headaches and put her in the hospital for further testing. Now this is where it gets interesting. He admitted my daughter to the hospital for tests, including a CT scan. She was put into a ward, a room with several beds in it with curtains separating each bed or unit.

Next to us was an older girl around 18 years old. Her mother had her admitted because of dreams and tremors. When this happened, she spoke in another voice in another language, and her whole body shook all over. This mother just wanted to make sure her daughter was in good health for she had never spent a day in the hospital except for the day she was born. I listened to her and thought good health speaking another language and body shaking all over? She was a little unbalanced in my book. Then the doctors came to see her, she explained what was happening to her daughter, and the doctors laughed right in her face. I felt bad for her until at just about the same moment in time, something interesting happened... the young women went into one of her fits, and suddenly I saw her feet shaking outside of the curtain, and the doctors ran to her bed side in order to check on her, and I heard this deep voice but did not understand anything that she was saying.

The doctors came out of her area, their faces white with shock and insisted that she be sent out for a CT scan stat! At that time, there were only a few CT scans around, and you were shipped out of the hospital to them for testing. The mother and daughter were fine with everything, and once again, they stated they just wanted proof that she was healthy and that nothing showed up on the scan. I still did not understand all of what was going on, but it would not be long before they let me in on their secret. My daughter was scheduled the next day for her scan.

When the young woman came back from her scan the doctors told her the scan looked good, but they were going to do a few more tests on her tomorrow, they were thoroughly confused. The young woman's mother asked me what my daughter was in for, and I told her what was happening and about her dreams. I saw the way her daughter looked at her as I was telling the story. She looked at her mother and said should we tell her mom? Her mother said NO! I asked what they were talking about, and she said nothing. I asked why her daughter was here? I understood what she was going through, but I did not understand why they kept telling me they were just ruling out that she was not sick. How could she not be sick when this was happening to her? The mother shared with me that her daughter got visions of a space ship. When she slept it came and took her body up into it, and now they talk through her. Woo... I felt like I was in the Twilight Zone. Lord help me... and yet something rang true about all this. They were both strong, and they believed that she was well and that this was really happening to her. Of course, they did not share this with the doctors. However, they did share this with me, why? They asked me more questions about my daughter about her dreams, so I proceeded to tell them the story. Again, the daughter kept looking at her mother, and again, she asked her, to only hear her reply of no. The mother asked me what I thought would happen if my daughter opened the door? I did not hesitate. I knew if my daughter opened the door to the man in black my daughter would die....this broke my heart because I felt so alone with all of this, and I had no way to prevent it.

How could I help my daughter? I had prayed and asked God to help me, and I knew he was the only one who could help me for this was way out of my league. The young women looked at her mother and said mom we have to tell her, and they went back and forth. Finally, I said, tell me what? If you have something to tell me that will help my child PLEASE tell me! The mother asked me if I would listen to what she had to say and follow everything she said, and if my daughter would listen to her daughter and do what she says. I was desperate and somewhere inside me I knew my answer was right here before my very eyes, sitting next to me in a hospital room. So the mother wrote down on a piece of paper what I was supposed to do at home and her daughter would work with my daughter that night in the hospital. I told my daughter to do whatever she was told to do. I did this in blind faith because somehow I knew it was the right thing to do. My daughter needed to repeat some words that were said to her. I went home that night and did my part while my daughter did hers. I could not wait to get back to the hospital the next morning to see what had happened and I was greeted by the biggest smile on my daughters face. She had slept for the first time in months all night long with no nightmares or night terrors.

It worked!! God had answered my prayers... I looked from one to another and all three were smiling at me. I was in tears. How could this be I asked? I was told to start reading Edgar Cayce's books. Who is he I asked? I soon found out. I was also asked if I would like to join a group that they belonged to, and I said no I was not ready for that yet (it kind of scared me).

How could I find them or these groups I asked? I was told that they were hidden because people were not ready for them to come out, and many people were scared of the things that they did not understand. How does someone find you if they need you, I asked? I was told. We find you.... Just like we did here... Then I was told that I must NEVER share this story with anyone, and I took that to heart.

I want to share with you that my daughter never had another nightmare. Her headaches were much better. In fact, it was not until a couple of years ago that we were all in the car with my daughter, who is now in her thirties, and my granddaughter was talking about a dream she had, and I made a comment at least it wasn't a nightmare like your mom use to have. My daughter looked at me and said what nightmare's mom? I said you have to be kidding. You don't remember them, and she said no. She wanted me to tell her about them, and I said no way! If you don't remember them, I'm sure not going to remind you of them.

Well, this bothered her and then later she came to me and said she was thinking about it, and little things started to come back to her, and she remembered the man in black. The reason being her daughter started having night terrors. So I shared and nipped that in the bud. I never told her all of it but I did share the how and what to do for it. Like I said I never shared this story until a few years ago.

Why now you ask? The answer is simple; the people are ready to hear. How do I know this? Because when I had my little store, parents were coming out of the woodwork sharing their horrifying stories with me about their children and their night terrors and not knowing what to do to help them. I could no longer sit and listen and do nothing to help these children and their families. I was there, and I experienced the horror and helplessness of not being able to help my own child. I was not going to let others suffer for fear of not sharing what happened to mine. I know it was not time then, but that was over thirty years ago. People hid because others were afraid.

Now is a new time, a Spiritual Awakening for all that are interested in getting on board. So I came out of my fear base, and I started to share with people what to do with their children. I wrote it out and told them to go home and follow the instructions. The success rate was over whelming. People were calling me and thanking me, writing letters and sending cards of thanks. The one that touched my heart was the mom that thanked me and told me she finally has her daughter back. I know how that feels.

I still remember, as if it were yesterday. I knew when I wrote this book that I was to put this story in it for everyone to read. I cannot reach enough children just by word of mouth so I am writing the words down as they were given to me, so that you may be able to help your own child or someone else's child.

As I go to my purse and pull out my wallet for this is where I have kept this precious piece of paper on me at all times. I think how it has transferred from every wallet, and every purse that I have ever had for the last thirty some years. Could you imagine how this paper looks about now? WORN OUT and very much loved and looked after. I placed a few pieces of tape on it for the first time ever, because I didn't want to lose what God had brought forth to save my child. Below are the words and instructions. We will call it the Prayer of Grace...or is it Salvation...

Before E-mail God

Answered Knee mail.

By Unknown

Chapter 25

Prayer of Grace

First and one of the most important things to do is to learn and say The Lord's Prayer (Our Father) with your child. Have them repeat the words after you. If they are older, they can say it by themselves if they wish. Now after they go to bed and when they are sleeping. The parent must go to another room and the first thing they must do is say the (Our Father) prayer. Then ask for Gods Protection - His Guidance - and his Strength. Then see yourself and surround yourself with the White Light of Christ. Then surround your child with the White Light of Christ. Then call out your child's name from the other room, they will not hear you but their Soul will. Identify yourself as their mother or father (as if you were speaking to them) - tell them everything is all right - tell them that God loves them very much - he is guiding you - protecting you - and his light surrounds you - tell them you love them - assure them everything is alright - at the end be sure to tell them to go back to sleep. (You are talking to their Souls)

It is that simple... God works in miraculous ways not difficult ways. Please share this with everyone who is in need, children and adults alike. I feel a kind of peace enter me NOW that I have shared this story. Now, it's in everyone's hand, and I thank the mother and daughter who shared this beautiful gift with me and gave my daughter back to me.

Child your words are of truth and need to be shared by those that are waiting for the words. God sent them to you as he sent you your earth angels in a time of need. Now it is time for the other earth angels to do their bidding and make sure the words spread, and the children heal, for all mankind needs to heal. We thank you for sharing. You have been released from your pledge. You are Free. Everyone is Free to share the words of our Father. For it is time.

*The Lords Prayer**

Our Father which art in heaven,

Hallowed be thy name.

Thy kingdom come.

Thy will be done on earth,

As it is in heaven.

Give us this day our daily bread.

And forgive us our trespasses,

As we forgive those that trespass against us

And lead us not into temptation,

But deliver us from evil:

For thine is the kingdom,

And the power, and the glory, for ever.

Amen.

That was difficult for me to write. I am not the best

story teller, and I know I could have told it better, but the problem is I really don't know how. Even so, I continue to write because the words need to be heard. Thank goodness Spirit tells a better story then I.

Chapter 26

Spirit Steps In

Dr. Laurence steps in as I sit this day in prayer. Who is Dr. Laurence you ask? It really doesn't matter what the name is, what does matter is the way I feel as this Spirit's energy enters my being? When I feel this power of love and strength come flooding through, it always sets me back just a bit wondering what is going to be said today. I thank God for this journey I am on, knowing full well he will send those to me that will fill this book with his Love and Desire with the words that will fill the voids of the many.

We cry for the want of universal peace. So many say they want it and yet they are afraid to make the steps to receive it. We look at the person our Father the universal being has created and we shake our heads wondering what went wrong and yet we know the answer to this question. God our father gave each one of you freedom of choice.

Ego has replaced it and what a word that has come to be. It is as if a person is divided in two pieces right down the middle. Love and Ego.. Peace and Ego.. Harmony and Ego.. Love, Peace and Harmony go together so nicely. Ego, EGO and EGO only grow one way and get in your way. It is the want of things, the control of things, and the best of things. It is all about YOU. It is harmful, devastating, and so controlling. It takes over and blossoms into GREED. If we could take that word and do away with it or replace it with a word that would show Respect, Pride, Goodness, Honesty, Sharing, Love, we might come back to Harmony. Your world is on very shaky grounds with all that is happening. The power of goodness is being replaced with ego, the want of which we have already discussed in the book. The earth is cleansing itself of the bad, useless and the unwanted. Mother earth is crying and trying to clean herself up. She is chasing her tail as others keep dumping their selfishness onto her. You see changes every day. You worry and wonder what is next, yet you keep repeating and repeating the same-old things. Changes have to occur in order for Harmony to settle in. Ego has to be pushed aside, and thoughts have to go out to others for you to be able to receive what is in store for all. Only those that are willing to give will be able to receive. The outcome is what you make it. It always has been and will continue to be so. Look around you and see what is happening to your world. Look around you and see what you have done to help make this happen. Now look around you and see what you can do to make some changes, to bring Harmony back into your lives.

We have registered that people are followers. They want what everyone else has, and then they want more. It does not matter the consequences. For they look no further, just, a step ahead of themselves. They do not feel they are hurting anyone it is just about them (ego) their want of it. Whether it is a thing, or success, the want of, they go for it, and they keep going even though they are never fulfilled. They forgot how to connect. They forgot how to find peace; they forgot how to stand still for just a moment of time and feel. Feel what life is really all about. It is not about the want of things, it is not about the power to control. It is about the energy of the universe, about the love of the people, about sharing, about the smiles on children's faces as they look at you, it's about family, world peace and the need of awakening your spiritual soul and walking forward in Gods light to find the peace you have been craving and denying yourself of for so long. It's about slowing down and looking around and really seeing what you have been missing. See the light as it enfolds you in its glory of healing, protecting and advancing into the goodness of everything.

Another WOW moment as always one of truth...

If truth be told many want what we have spoken about and many are just too selfish and caught up in their own lives to take the time to stop and look because they are afraid that they will get left behind. So they continue to rush and push ahead without thought of anyone else because they have been programmed to do just that. It is as if walking with blinders on and not acknowledging anyone in their path. They forget to smile or say good day, they just go on their way. While in the long run they miss out on the purpose of why they came to your earth plane to begin with. It's called growth but not necessarily the way you have been designed to think of it.

Chapter 27

Growth

From the very first moment, you were conceived you had a destiny planned out for you. Several in fact... The one you picked on the other side before you came here, the one your parents wanted for you, and the one you formed within your own life. In many cases, you got confused and reprogrammed by the people you met, by peer pressure and sometimes just by your own stubbornness, and the want of it. There it is again... The want of... it is not always a bad thing because it can give *you the determination you need in life to carry you through. You come to this earth plane with a clear slate knowing you have certain things to accomplish in order for growth. What happens in between the time you're born, and you get to the age where you are now to accomplish all of these things? Many years, many people telling you what and how to do it, confusion sets in and along the way you get lost. Then it takes time to find you once again and sometimes this takes years. Years of your life and you feel like you will never find what it is you are looking for, yet you know not what you look for. Sound like something you have been through?*

As you get older your asking yourself, what am I going to be when I grow up? You feel like a kid inside but when you look in the mirror, you see an older face looking back at you. What's going on here, this can't be me? However, you feel your body getting weaker and your bones not standing as tall and strong as they use to be. You're looking at things a little differently. You came in as a helpless child, and you feel yourself going down the same road, yet differently. As a mature adult you have choices now that you never had as a child. You can see and think differently. You can make things happen and change things that you no longer wish to be a part of.

You have come to that crossroad in your life where you can make the difference in the outcome. For some, growth may take a little longer but when you step up to the plate and realize that you only have so much time left to accomplish your task,(even if you have no idea what that task is) you tend to look at things a little differently. You see things with your eyes open, no longer are you willing to close them to the unkindness of humanity. You wish to leave this world of yours with as much glory as possible. This is when real growth sets in. This is when you see yourself for what you are and where you have been, and for what you have done.

This is when you feel guilty for all the wrong you have accomplished in your life. This is when you want to change and make changes for all to be right in your world. You want people to remember you for the good not the bad, you want them to smile when they think of you, not frown. What we see as, growth comes to many, in many different forms, some out of guilt and others out of a newness that has taken over their being. You see you come to this place on earth to develop, to learn and grow into the person you were meant to be. You experience many different choices along the way, and this is also for growth. You are not all Angels here on this earth plane. Some have made very bad choices only to redo and learn from. How can you learn if everything is always good? You must experience the bad and ugly for you to know the good and beautiful.

For growth, you must water the plant to see it grow. You must feed the plant in order to watch it grow. You must give it plenty of sunshine for it to grow. You are the plant. You came to earth to grow. You are given the things you need to grow. Some are slow growers because they have not received or been given what it is they need, to grow nice and strong. You are fortunate to be human and not a plant that relies on others *for their growth.*

You and only you can make the steps that you need for the growth that you conceive. You came here for a reason. Look inside yourself and ask. What have I come here for? What is it, I need to know or do in order for the growth I need? You will find real growth when you find peace. To find peace you must give of your services to those in need. You must help others to grow so they will be stronger rather than weaker. You must reach out your hand to those around you and give of yourself. You must shed a tear for those that are hurt or wounded and give them the strength they need. You must show them that they are loved and needed in this society of yours. You must speak the word of your Father and let them know they are children of the Lord, your neighbors, your salvation.

You must all come together in unity for there to be world peace. This can only be done one person at a time over and over again until everyone everywhere hears and knows the power of redemption. For that is where Growth will be found.

As I read your words, I exhale a deep breath for your words hit a spot so deep within me that I realized I had been holding my breath the whole time I was reading your words. It is so much for us to take in. Let's take a look at the word "REDEMPTION" a big power word. What exactly does it mean? I pulled up the dictionary and here is the definition: (Improving of something: The saving or improving of something that has declined into a poor state.) Yep that's us alright. What do you say, should we try saving and improving our world? Let us redeem what has been taken from us.

Chapter 28

Suicide

The killing of oneself that is what the dictionary says; written in black and white. Plain as day, it is wrong, the bible states it so. Condemn the person, judge them, give them a sentence, a punishment, blame, it is wrong and unacceptable.

Yes, I could agree with some of that, but to a certain point. When someone is depressed, they know not what they do. Should we condemn them? I think not. There are many reasons I say this. When I had my store, I use to get a lot of people walking through my doors looking for help. For awhile it seemed that every other person that came to me for a reading was contemplating suicide, thinking of taking their life. They felt it was not worth living any more, yet they must have still wanted to live, or they would not have been coming to see me for a reading. What I did not realize was how desperate these people were.

They were searching for something without knowing what or how they were going to receive it. That included me... I remember once working a fair, a young woman came in with her boyfriend or so I thought. She looked around and sat down at my table. I remember her as being beautiful to look at yet I could feel sadness, as soon as she sat down and joined me

When I do a reading I always ask God to give me the words that his child needs to hear. I felt the presence of spirit enter my body and start to speak to her. This does not usually occur at a fair, but I let it flow and these words came out of my mouth. Don't do it! I should never have taken my life. It was wrong. I know it now. I had so much to live for, and now it has all been taken away from me. Please... please do not follow me here because we will not be together. You need to live your life. You need to remember me not as I was, but as I should have been. Stronger. I love you. PLEASE DON'T DO IT..... This beautiful girl screamed jumped up out of her chair as it tipped over. She startled and scared the daylights out of me... I jumped up and we stood looking at each other. To say the least we were both surprised and startled from the message. I asked her to sit back down, and she started to cry as she told me about her boyfriend that had killed himself. She was lost without him, and she felt she could no longer live without him, so she was going to join him. I explained that he came to her to help her and let her know that she was not to follow through with her plans. That she would not be with him. She was grieving and she had a right to be very sad, but she did not have a right to end her life because of it. I also told her she had a wonderful life ahead of her just waiting for her to wake up and see clearly once again. When a person grieves, they can become very depressed and as depression sets in, they lose track of everything else including life and how precious, it is.

Many people walked through my doors losing love ones, including their children. Many became lost; forget about their spouses and other children in their families because all they focused on was the death of their little one. They cannot go forward, the pain is too great and all they can think about is to end their life in order to end their pain. However, at the same time giving pain to those that they leave behind to carry on.

The problem being is they cannot look forward. They do not see what lies ahead. They are consumed in grief, pain and misery. They need help neither judgment nor condemning. They need someone to step up to the plate and seek them the help that they need. Someone has to be responsible for the living. In my own way, I reach those that are sent to me. I help them to come back to the living even if it is painful. They must see that their loved ones are being taken care of on the other side. They must know that they can still talk to them and feel them in a whole new way. What they miss is the human form, the love, the touch, the hugs and smiles.

We as humans are selfish and do not want to release our children and loved ones. We want them to stay with us forever. As a mother and wife, I feel the same way, and I will grieve when my loved ones depart, but I will stay with the living for I know they will join me more easily than if I gave up on life. It is not an easy thing I speak of for I have lost loved ones, and I feel the loss of so many others when they seek me out to comfort them. Love is a very precious private gift that we give to another being. To lose that we lose part of who we are, just as if we have lost a limb. We must rebuild our lives without them in it. This consists of many unpleasant things that we must do. What everyone must realize is that life is a precious gift that has been given to us and we must take each day as if it is the last, because we do not know how many more we may have.

We come into this world carrying our burdens one after another. When it gets too heavy, some crack, mentally, emotionally and spiritually. Once again, lives are taken and once again not really on a conscious level or thought. It just happens. As if you are reading a story that becomes a nightmare, and you find yourself part of that story and not knowing how to get out of it or even if you can get out of it. You just know that you have to end the nightmare that you have become a part of. So you take the life that feels tortured and end the story. I have seen it, felt it and become part of it. It feels like a dream. You see it happening, but you can't stop it. You have no control as if someone else has stepped into your being and taken control of your limbs and taken it into their own hands. This is a scary but so true. So the next time you say unkind words when you hear someone has taken their life think again and send a prayer out to that person and send him or her to the light, that they may find their way back home once again.

I used to ask Spirit, why do you bring these people to me? It used to scare me. I was frightened that I would not be able to help them. How foolish was I? For you see I was not alone in this. Spirit was right there beside me giving me the words to give and helping them to receive in the manner which they needed. This was not about me, and I always need to remember that. It is not about what I feel; it is about putting myself out there with trust and give of what I receive to those in need.

Many people think death will take them away from pain but what they do not realize is, pain is part of growth. Many are very fragile at this time in your world today. They crack very easily like an egg that is not handled gently. They run for cover. They hide. They hold all their sorrow in until they come crashing down. We watch, we observe and we try to help as much of mankind as we can. Nevertheless, we see a wedge being construed, and it gets more difficult to get through. People are running away and hiding their feelings not letting others in order to help. They feel no one is there for them. This is a way out of their misery, an escape. What they must become aware of is there is no escape, for it just follows them to the other side. The truly emotionally unstable ones we take aside and help them to recover. The ones that do it for the ego sake must continue through until they discover the wrong in their ways and must make amends to continue in their growth. For you see there is always growth whether it is here or there. The ones that are left behind are the ones that truly suffer. For they have no understanding why their loved ones chose to take their life. They grieve for them looking for the why. Always searching and wondering, thinking they could have helped when in all reality, there was not a thing they could have done. For all of you that have lost a loved one or friend in this way, please know that they will receive what it is they feel they are missing in life. They will gather as children and see the wrongs of their ways. They will make amends to each of you but most of all to themselves will they be true. This we know through the Spirit of Christ.

Thank you for the understanding of what happens to those we love. We always hear stories like they will burn in hell. They will suffer eternally forever. I always believed that God put us here for growth and through are mistakes we grow. This is a huge mistake, but with all mistakes comes growth so why not this also. People react differently to suicide. It's considered a mortal sin if you are Catholic. Religion plays a big part in people's reactions. I think the biggest part is played by God not man. So the way I see it is God will handle all are mistakes and help us to purify what it is we have done wrong in our lives. Suicide is NEVER the answer and will never be the answer. So please do not threaten your life with something that is going to hurt the ones you love. There is always another way. It may be harder, and you may have to work at it or suffer through it, but in the long run it is the easiest escape there is, living life to the fullest.

Chapter 29

Today is the day...

Today as in every day you may come up against a solid wall of agony. Someone somewhere is going to throw something at you that you cannot catch. In the long run, it will get dented up by the time of retrieval.

I have watched and seen adults who are too afraid to come out of their safe area with a shell they have built for themselves. For they still hold on to the fear of childhood and are to afraid to take a chance and reach outside their comfort zone to experience what the world has to offer them now. We are no longer children. We are adults having a child's experience. Yet in God's eyes we are his children. He graces us with his attention and love, as a parent does to his child. We did not all have a rosy childhood. We were not all happy growing up. Some of us carry such sad fearful memories its, as if we are stepping back in time. Remembering the horror, the pain, and the sadness and wondering how we survived and still wondering how we continue yet this day. Looking back and then looking at life now some things seem not to have changed. A pattern may have developed not because you wanted it to, but you knew no other way. Others are running as fast and as far as they can to get away from it, yet it never goes away. It's with you. And still others walked the walk and face the demons and are in the survival mode of life and looking ahead to make changes and to grow in strength.

In this line of work, I do see grown adults sit down across from me, and then I see the scared child that emerges from their being. Sometimes it is difficult to know if I am reading for the child or adult. In most cases, it is for both. For the struggle continues... I'll hear responses coming out of them. *"My father killed himself. I'm so afraid that I will follow in his footsteps"*... that's all he thinks about! Why? *"My husband shot himself and left me all alone to raise our family." "Why didn't he talk to me, share with me?" "My wife died, and I have no reason to go on living."* He does not know how to live without her. *"My child was in a terrible accident and died. She has left us." "I no longer can go on. My husband and I no longer communicate." "It has destroyed us." "What do I do? How do I survive?" "Do I even want to continue? "The pain hurts... it hurts so bad. It would be so much easier to just give up!"* These are only some of the words I hear. However, what I really hear is... the hurt, the pain, the anger, the loss of a loved one. They are scared of the loneliness and the emptiness of their today's and tomorrow's. The memories how joyful they once were are now PAINFUL.

Like a child, they have fallen, and they must get up carefully or continue to live and watch their life slip by with no meaning, no love, no kindness, and no life. Each step that is taken, is taken carefully like a child just learning to walk. They toddle this way and that, weave back and forth hands out to balance themselves and when they breakdown (fall down) they must push themselves back up and start all over again, until they get stronger and more sure of themselves. Until they can walk, then run and then play once again. God put beautiful flowers on this Earth to grow, pick, smell, and display and then go back into the earth. He also put a seed into that flower to fall to the ground and to start growing all over again.

It makes perfect sense when you compare yourself to a flower. They are unique, beautiful, fragile and needing nourishment to continue the growth and to multiply. To be compared to a flower I never quite thought of it in that term before, yet it makes perfect sense. Life is but a flower, and yet it withers and dies. Even so, while it is around it sure makes an impression. We give flowers to others for many different occasions. Birthdays, Sweetest Day, Valentine's Day, Anniversaries, yet we also communicate with flowers at Funerals and take them to place at Cemeteries. We use flowers for LOVE. We express LOVE through the beauty of flowers. A bouquet of flowers: the looks, the smell, the gathering of so many yet different kinds together as a whole. We are expressing once again the love we have and want to share with others.

Now take people, do you not see all of us as flowers. Some tall, some short, some pretty, some plain, some smelly and others just put in order to fill the space with a happy face. When you look at people try to imagine them as flowers and a purpose to be here. Imagine what kind they are and what gift, they give to you and to another's and what do they receive from each individual. This is not a game. It puts your intention in another place. To see, to feel and to know everyone that God puts here attached to mother earth is but a flower that very well does leave seeds behind to grow and develop all over again.

Everyone is always trying new brands, mixing species, trying to develop new colors, until we get all mixed up with names, colors and fragrances. What happened to the old and standard beauty, the Red Rose? Now we have at least half-dozen different types of red rose. Were are confused, the directions have been thrown away. We are in search. How do we know what is best and how to grow it any longer? We no longer go to a green house. We go to a grocery store. Life is a short, one-stop shop. We have forgotten the beauty of the red rose

Life is short, and we are forgetting the beauty of all, we are forgetting to breathe. Many of us catch are breath, hold our breath. In meditation class the first thing, I say to my students is to breathe. Become aware of your breath. Someone comes to me with a problem I say BREATHE, Some ones up set, I say BREATHE. Anxiety BREATHE...

Breath is so important, and we take it for granted until we can't breathe.

Our bodies function on their own, they are smart. Our brains have the capabilities to do everything that it needs to do in order to work properly. We are the ones that confuse it and abuse it. We are like a spinning top and while it's spinning the energy works beautifully. However, once it runs out of energy, it falls to the floor to be picked up once again to be spun. Now imagine your body, see what food you ingest and the fuel that it needs is not always what you put in it. The energy is not there to work or function properly. Rest, what is that?, a new word. Not in our dictionary; to rest our bodies with proper sleep. I know for one that is not on my agenda. I, like so many others am tired all the time... where did my energy go? Why can't I feel like I did when I was younger? We all know the answer, but we do not want to be responsible for the problem or outcome. If only we treated ourselves like we treat others all would be so much easier. Then how could we complain and blame another. What a wonderful world we live in, we have so much offered to us in any quantity we want, and we abuse it. We give ourselves permission to overindulge in STUFF.

Because we feel we deserve it when we know that it will only hurt us in the long run. I am right there at the top of the list looking at my life through a microscope. The changes I want to make and the changes I will make are not always the same. We shortchange ourselves and belittle ourselves into believing what we say to alter the situation. When it comes to working on ourselves, we are tired, we are lazy, and we are inconsiderate, because we can be. Because we work so hard for others, we don't want to work that hard for ourselves. SHAME ON US! It is time for all of us to start kicking some butt... that would be our own butts... we need to start delivering what it is we need into our lives, NOW... TODAY... not tomorrow. We need to make changes in our lives. We need to start smiling more, laughing more and loving, who we are, for us, not someone else. So we can be the recipient and know how it feels to love ourselves and to be free, not only give but to receive the gifts that were meant to be given to us.

Wow I always have a hard time with that, and I am weak just as many of you are. However, I am working up my appetite, so I may consider what is useful in my life and what is not. I am looking at my life a little differently today than I did yesterday. I am going forward in smaller steps and finishing up what I started and completing what it is that I need to get done for me. In this way and only this way will I feel the balance in my life coming back to me once again.

I know how I feel when I complete something. I feel whole. I feel like I'm someone, I feel totally embraced in feelings that I don't get to touch very often. I want to feel good about myself, and I want to touch those feelings more often because I need to prove to myself how important I am to ME.... If and only when I do this for myself will I be able to fully give of myself to another in true being and true oneness. Thank you God for this gift of oneness with myself and you, for we are One.

Chapter 30

The End Or Is It Just The Beginning?

I'm looking at my desk the one that called to me wondering if I had accomplished what I was sent to do? All I know is that life is a wonderful journey and yet a very complicated process. I also know that since I have connected with Spirit it has helped me to develop who and what I am. It has helped me in my everyday life as well as looking to the future with peace in my heart. Will it always be good? I doubt it, but it will be the best that I can do, and I do believe that God allows us to walk our walk, and he also helps us in the process. With God by our side how can we go wrong? The only way I figure it is if we don't let him in. I for one will leave the door open and pray that he joins me every step of the way. As I stand here and push the chair back under the desk, I know deep in my heart, I have done what I needed to do. I shared my story with you. Now I can continue to grow in the newness of life. For our work is never done. There are so many people out in our world looking for answers and never quite finding what it is they are looking for. I know you have a story to share but have never thought to put it out in the universe where people can reach it.

Now is the time for all good people to come to their senses and reach out to the universal power of all good and speak of the heart and soul that others may be reached. We are waiting and anticipating what the future holds for all of us. Let's turn the pages and give the universe what it needs. Love, Harmony and the Truth of Honesty. No more fear based society for me. Turn off the news and let them know we want happy, turn off the screaming talk shows and let them know we want harmony and laughter. Take hold of the old and give it a toss and grab hold of the new and allow it to be. We want Freedom to choose God in our lives once again. For with him by our side we will be a society of wealth. Not always in material things but in togetherness and sharing as a whole as we were meant to be. Not you and I against the world but you and I for the world, my world, your world, OUR WORLD.

Kathy is a Michigan resident, who discovered her ability to connect with Spirit in her early years.
Now a mother of four, who spends a lot of her time loving her eleven grandchildren?

Kathy and her husband Michael, their rescue cat - Destiny and Yorkie-Sashay, spend their weekends by the river at their little retreat up north to stay balanced.

Even with her full plate, Kathy found the time to write her first book *Butterfly Within* and now *Stop the Children from Crying a River of Tears*.

Kathy teaches Meditation, Intuitive Development, Reiki and Quantum-Touch Healing classes.

Kathy is a Hypnotist, Medium, and Spiritual Reader who has spoken at Baker College; many women's groups and events. She has been featured in various magazines and newspapers; such as Concepts Magazine the Macomb Daily and Detroit Free Press Newspaper.

She believes each day is a blessing to be used for growth.

http://KathyGarbe.com

http://facebook.com/StoptheChildrenfromCrying